BILTMORE™

OUR TABLE TO YOURS

Chef's Selection Cookbook

BILTMORE™

OUR TABLE TO YOURS
Chef's Selection Cookbook

Published by The Biltmore Company
One North Pack Square
Asheville, North Carolina 28801
828-225-1422

Copyright © 2007 The Biltmore Company

PHOTOGRAPHY: Cover and food page photography © Mike Rutherford
Botanicals on pages 13, 51, 89, and 127 © Visual Language
All additional photography © The Biltmore Company

BILTMORE CONTRIBUTORS
World Class Culinary Staff
Curatorial/Museum Services Staff
Marketing Staff

Library of Congress Catalog Number: 2006938740
ISBN: 978-1-885378-20-0

Edited, Designed, and Manufactured by
Favorite Recipes® Press
An imprint of

FRP™

P.O. Box 305142
Nashville, Tennessee 37230
800-358-0560

ART DIRECTOR: Steve Newman
BOOK DESIGN: Brad Whitfield & Susan Breining
EDITORIAL DIRECTOR: Mary Cummings
PROJECT EDITOR: Jane Hinshaw
PROJECT COORDINATORS: Ashley Bienvenu & Debbie Van Mol
FOOD STYLIST: Mary Ann Fowlkes

Manufactured in China
First Printing 2007 40,000

Biltmore Estate is open 365 days a year. For information about Biltmore Estate,
tickets, or Inn on Biltmore Estate reservations, call 800-543-2961 or
visit our Web site at www.biltmore.com.

To purchase additional copies of this book, please call 800-968-0558.

Contents

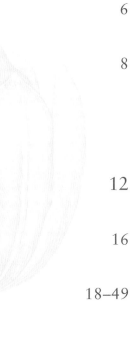

Preface

From its beginning as a private country estate to its current designation as a National Historic Landmark, Biltmore remains authentic and inspiring while setting the standard for gracious hospitality, attention to detail, and a welcoming attitude that captures the spirit of George and Edith Vanderbilt.

Guests of the Vanderbilt Family were celebrated in the finest style at Biltmore. Sometimes that meant a telegram to New York City requesting that a shipment of Blue Point oysters—

or some other exotic delicacy—be sent on the overnight train that stopped in Asheville. More often, however, guests enjoyed the bounty of the estate itself, including fresh beef and poultry; dairy products from the estate's prize-winning Jersey herd; and a wide variety of fruits and vegetables. In fact, according to an 1897 article from The Asheville News and Hotel Reporter, *"The Biltmore Gardens enjoy the reputation for the earliest vegetables and the largest variety of garden delicacies which are a little better, a little larger, and more in season than those of its competitors."*

We have remained true to our agricultural traditions even as we expand our legacy to include more dining options on the property, as well as our portfolio of award-winning Biltmore wines. In keeping with my great-grandparents' desire to provide the very best for their guests, I am proud to say that Biltmore is still a working farm that continues to offer the cream of the crop to our guests today. I encourage you to bring Biltmore to your table with each of these estate-inspired recipes created by our own chefs— perfect for every taste, every season, and every occasion.

Bill Cecil, Jr.

BILL CECIL, JR.
President & CEO
The Biltmore Company

Introduction

Biltmore Estate has always been a working, self-sufficient estate supported by diverse farming operations. When George Washington Vanderbilt (1862–1914) first envisioned his estate in the late 1880s, agriculture in the mountains of North Carolina was primitive and suffered from years of misguided land management practices. Vanderbilt was committed to bringing new knowledge and farming technology to the region. The following excerpts from the article "Farmer Vanderbilt," which appeared in The Asheville News and Hotel Report on February 20, 1897, summarize Mr. Vanderbilt's contributions to Western North Carolina agriculture.

"Everyone is familiar with the famous Biltmore Mansion and boundless estate of the young millionaire but to only a few is known the wonderful development of his farm which only a few years ago was comparatively a wilderness. It is Vanderbilt the farmer, not Vanderbilt of the Chateau, who has proven to be the great benefactor of Western North Carolina. He has shown the Carolinians the productive capacities of their virgin soil (that great mine of wealth they have profited by so little) by the scientific drainage, the improved machinery, the importation of fine stock, the judicious and lavish use of fertilizers, and the most up-to-date and scientific methods of farming that have characterized the management of the farm from the beginning."

"Anyone who knew the barren hills, the washed rut gullies, sedge fields, swamps, ditches, and the succession of worn out farms with their tumbledown houses—in which their owners were starving—that a short while ago occupied the site of the now splendid and fertile Biltmore Estate is struck with amazement at the marvelous change that has been wrought by the

wise expenditure of money on the most desirable and beautiful location in the world. This plantation is destined to become far more widely known than the Chateau because a house as magnificent as Vanderbilt's can be built anywhere, but only in Western North Carolina can be found such a naturally advantageous location as this. And even here cannot be found another place like this one."

From the beginning, farming and farm families comprised the heart and soul of Biltmore Estate's agricultural operations, which included a poultry farm, sheep herd, piggery, and a prize-winning herd of purebred Jersey dairy cows. The establishment of Biltmore Dairy put the estate on the map, as well as on the doorstep of almost every home in North Carolina. The dairy employed hundreds of estate workers over the years and became famous for its milk, cream, butter, and ice cream.

Fields across the estate also yielded tomatoes, strawberries, cabbage, carrots, lettuce, corn, sweet potatoes, melons, and greens. Apple orchards flourished as did other native fruit trees—persimmon, pawpaw, and fig. Biltmore's apiary produced sourwood and crimson clover honey. Game was plentiful as well and yielded meals for the hunters' sideboards of wild turkey, pheasant, venison, and boar.

Vanderbilt married Edith Stuyvesant Dresser (1873–1958) in 1898. When the couple entertained family and friends, and this happened often, a highlight of the stay was dining on products fresh from the farm. Each day, Biltmore's chef created a ledger of menus that were presented to Mrs. Vanderbilt, who approved, and occasionally improved upon, the many courses proposed for a single dining experience. The pantries and kitchens inside Biltmore House were constantly busy with the smells from the rotisserie and pastry kitchen wafting bewitchingly throughout the house. Silver was polished, crystal carefully washed and dried, and fine French linens laundered and pressed.

As evening approached and the Banquet Hall table was set with gleaming china, crystal, and silver against a backdrop of roaring fires in the room's triple fireplace, the effect was dazzling. Ladies appeared in the latest French gowns, while gentlemen were outfitted in fine tailored formal attire. Liveried butlers stood by attentively, anticipating every wish and need as guests savored each exquisite combination of courses and lively conversation.

This is the picture of entertaining at Biltmore House in the late 1890s that most of us imagine, and it is accurate. But consider the robust workings of the estate, its many farm and dairy families and residents or the every day enjoyments of the Vanderbilts with their young daughter Cornelia Stuyvesant Vanderbilt (1900–1976). Suppers across the property were plentiful, tables laden with the bounty of Biltmore. School lunches were prepared. Picnics for the Vanderbilts and their guests were packed in hampers and loaded onto carriages. Farm wives delighted in baking and canning competitions at the annual fall fair. Mrs. Vanderbilt brought soup to the workers' families during outbreaks of illness. Hunting trips to the Vanderbilts' Buck Spring Lodge on Mt. Pisgah meant conveying weeks' worth of food by horseback and wagon.

At the heart of all of these activities at Biltmore was an appreciation of food and drink as a genuine expression of welcome and hospitality, home, and hearth. Today, Biltmore continues this tradition with its commitment to the table as a place where family and friends gather, share ideas and opinions, and most importantly, create memories. In this spirit, Biltmore chefs are sharing more than 150 of their favorite original recipes in this collection. The offerings reflect the diversity of Biltmore's past and present, from homegrown mountain food to elegant entrées fit for a Vanderbilt.

Today, many of the same traditions continue. Biltmore features estate-raised beef and lamb, as well as a variety of vegetables and fruits from our kitchen garden, in our restaurants. As a producer of fine wines, Biltmore is also expanding its definition of gracious living by creating grand vintages to complement a white tablecloth dining experience as well as a collection of wines to make a weeknight meal seem grand. Enjoy them in your own manor with one of the recipes featured in Biltmore™: Our Table To Yours. And each time you do, raise a toast to the finer things in life—your friends and family gathered around the table.

Spring in the North Carolina

mountains comes slowly,

tempting those who anticipate the

season to rise early and linger late,

savoring each day. Brooks begin

to trickle down the mountainsides

with the promise of new life as fresh,

pale green stems venture towards

the lengthening days of warm sunshine.

Spring

Spring

fresh, pale green stems venture towards

the lengthening days of warm sunshine.

The spectacular array of spring

blossoms throughout the gardens at

Biltmore is a kaleidoscope of color and

scent, a fresh and lively tribute to

Frederick Law Olmsted, the father of

landscape architecture in America.

His "gardens of ornament" are a

testament to George Vanderbilt's love

Spring in the North Carolina mountains

comes slowly, tempting those who anticipate

the season to rise early and linger late, savoring

each day. Brooks begin to trickle down the

mountainsides with the promise of new life as

of nature and appreciation of landscape. But it was the farm at Biltmore that always remained at the

center of George Vanderbilt's dream and supported his belief in the estate's self-sufficiency. In the late

1800s, Vanderbilt's farm managers imparted the knowledge of the most modern farming techniques to

the people of a region previously overworked and depleted. Estate workers put in spring crops, defying

late frosts and illustrating the mountaineers' hardiness and faithful optimism. The rewards at the table

were many: succulent sweet spring vegetables, the arrival of tender lamb, freshly caught mountain trout,

early wild strawberries, and fresh cream from Biltmore's Jersey cows. Gathering around the many tables

across the estate—both inside Biltmore House as well as in families' homes across the property—the

bounty of the land was blessed daily in the sweet light of a mountain spring.

Spring Lunch Menu

Smoked Trout Tartare
with Horseradish and Dill

Green and White Asparagus Salad
with Citrus Confit

Crisp Potato Pizza with
Sweet Peppers, Goat Cheese
and Olive Tapenade

Red Velvet Cake with
Cream Cheese Frosting

Lavender Martini

Smoked Trout Tartare with Horseradish and Dill

Carrot and Ginger Soup with Curried Crème Fraîche

2 onions, chopped
4 ribs celery, chopped
1/2 cup chopped garlic
1/4 cup (1/2 stick) butter, melted
4 pounds carrots, peeled and chopped
1/4 cup all-purpose flour
1 cup sherry
2 quarts (8 cups) chicken stock

3 tablespoons honey
1/2 cup minced peeled ginger
2 teaspoons chopped fresh thyme
3 tablespoons salt
2 teaspoons white pepper
2 cups heavy cream
Curried Crème Fraîche (below)

Sweat the onions, celery and garlic in the butter in a saucepan over low heat until translucent. Add the carrots and sauté until the carrots are tender. Sprinkle with the flour and cook for 2 minutes, stirring frequently. Add the sherry and cook until thickened, stirring constantly to deglaze the saucepan and to prevent lumps from forming. Cook until the liquid is reduced by 3/4.

Add the chicken stock, honey, ginger, thyme, salt and white pepper. Simmer for 20 to 30 minutes or until the desired consistency. Stir in the cream and adjust the seasoning. Cook just until heated through; do not boil. Ladle into soup bowls and top with a dollop of Curried Crème Fraîche.

Serves four to six

Wine Master's Suggestion: Biltmore Riesling

Curried Crème Fraîche

1 cup crème fraîche
1/2 teaspoon curry powder
pinch of salt

Combine the crème fraîche, curry powder and salt in a bowl and mix gently.

Serves four to six

Cornelia's Wedding Breakfast, April 1924

Cornelia Vanderbilt married the Hon. John Francis Amherst Cecil, a British diplomat, on April 24, 1924. The guest list included such familiar names as Astor, Waldorf Astoria, Condé Nast, Post, and Pulitzer, as well as official representatives from a dozen countries. Following the ceremony in All Soul's Church in Biltmore Village, nearly a thousand guests came to Biltmore House for a wedding breakfast. The couple dined in the Winter Garden at a horseshoe-shaped table graced with exquisite eighteenth-century silver from the foremost silversmiths of the time. Other guests enjoyed a buffet in the Banquet Hall.

The Winter Garden, 2004 photo

Surrounding the fountain sculpture Boy Stealing Geese by Austrian-American artist Karl Bitter is a re-creation of the bride's table from Cornelia's 1924 wedding.

Country Ham and Leek Strata

1 pound challah
1/3 pound unsalted butter, softened
2 tablespoons canola oil
16 ounces country ham, chopped into
    medium pieces
1 1/4 cups chopped leeks,
    white portions only
2 tablespoons chopped garlic
1 teaspoon dried thyme

1 teaspoon kosher salt
1/2 teaspoon pepper
4 cups (16 ounces) shredded
    Gruyère cheese
8 eggs, beaten
5 cups milk
1/4 teaspoon nutmeg
1 teaspoon kosher salt

Preheat the oven to 325 degrees. Cut the challah into slices 3/4 inch thick and cut the slices into halves. Spread both sides of the bread with the butter.

Heat a medium skillet over medium heat and add the canola oil and country ham. Cook for 1 minute. Add the leeks, garlic, thyme, 1 teaspoon kosher salt and the pepper. Cook for about 8 minutes or until the leeks are tender. Let stand until cool.

Layer half the bread slices closely together in a large buttered baking dish. Layer half the ham mixture and half the Gruyère cheese over the bread. Repeat the layers.

Combine the eggs, milk, nutmeg and 1 teaspoon kosher salt in a bowl and whisk until smooth. Pour over the layers. Place in a large pan with water reaching halfway up the sides of the baking dish. Bake for 30 minutes. Test to see if the center is set and continue to bake, testing every 10 minutes until set or until the center reaches an internal temperature of 140 degrees. Serve immediately.

Serves ten   *Wine Master's Suggestion*: Biltmore Cabernet Sauvignon Blanc de Noir

Carolina Crab Velouté

1/4 cup sliced shallots
1 teaspoon black peppercorns
1 bay leaf
2 tablespoons butter, melted
1 gallon crab stock
1 cup heavy cream
2 cups milk
1 1/2 tablespoons cornstarch
1/2 tablespoon sherry

1/2 tablespoon Worcestershire sauce
2 cups heavy cream
salt and white pepper to taste
2 tablespoons crab roe

Garnish
jumbo lump crab meat and chopped
    fresh chives

Sweat the shallots with the peppercorns and bay leaf in the butter in a soup pot over medium heat for 4 to 5 minutes or until the shallots are translucent. Add the crab stock and cook until reduced by 3/4.

Combine 1 cup cream with the milk in a saucepan and heat over low heat. Add the mixture to the crab stock mixture and bring to a simmer over medium-low heat.

Whisk the cornstarch, sherry and Worcestershire sauce in a small bowl until smooth. Stir into the simmering mixture and cook until thickened, stirring constantly; the mixture will thicken quickly. Cook over low heat for 10 to 15 minutes longer, stirring occasionally. Strain and return to the soup pot, discarding the solids.

Stir in 2 cups cream and season with salt and white pepper. Stir in the crab roe. Heat just to serving temperature. Ladle into soup bowls and garnish with jumbo lump crab meat and fresh chives.

Serves four to six   *Wine Master's Suggestion*: Biltmore Pinot Grigio

Smoked Trout Tartare with Horseradish and Dill

This tartare is wonderful served with grilled bread and thin slices of cucumber. If smoked trout is not available, smoked salmon would make a perfect substitute.

8 ounces cold smoked trout, skinned and trimmed
2 tablespoons minced red onion
1 tablespoon capers
1 tablespoon coarsely chopped fresh dill weed
1 1/2 teaspoons prepared horseradish
1/8 teaspoon grated lemon zest
1 teaspoon lemon juice
2 tablespoons sour cream
1/4 teaspoon Tabasco sauce
1/8 teaspoon pepper

Cut the trout into small dice. Combine with the onion, capers, dill weed and horseradish in a medium bowl. Add the lemon zest, lemon juice, sour cream, Tabasco sauce and pepper. Fold together gently, taking care not to overmix. Chill until serving time. Pack into individual molds if desired.

Be careful to grate only the colored portion of the skin of the lemon or other citrus fruits when zesting them, as the white portion between the skin and the meat is bitter.

Serves four

Wine Master's Suggestion:
Biltmore
Château Reserve
Chardonnay

Farmer Vanderbilt

An 1897 article entitled Farmer Vanderbilt *noted:*

The Biltmore Gardens enjoy the reputation for the earliest vegetables and the largest variety of garden delicacies, which are a little better, a little larger, and more in season than those of its competitors. In fact, it does better as a business than all others combined. At the State Fairs, the products of this farm rank high, and invariably take the first premiums when entered for that purpose. At every exposition there is a large exhibit which includes everything from a herd of registered Jerseys down to a basket of potatoes.

Green and White Asparagus Salad with Citrus Confit

Honey Mustard Vinaigrette
1/4 cup champagne vinegar
1 tablespoon honey
2 teaspoons Dijon mustard
1 1/2 teaspoons minced shallot
2 teaspoons chopped fresh thyme
3/4 cup vegetable oil
salt and pepper to taste

Salad
18 jumbo green asparagus spears
18 white asparagus spears
salt to taste
1 bunch watercress
1 head frisée
Citrus Confit (below)

For the vinaigrette, combine the vinegar, honey, Dijon mustard, shallot and thyme in a bowl and mix well. Add the oil gradually, whisking constantly to blend well. Season with salt and pepper.

For the salad, peel the asparagus. Bring a large saucepan of salted water to a boil. Add the asparagus and cook for 30 seconds or until the color brightens. Remove to a bowl of ice water to stop the cooking process; drain.

Cut the bottom stems from the watercress and frisée. Toss with some of the vinaigrette in a bowl and place on serving plates. Arrange 3 green and 3 white asparagus spears on each salad and drizzle with additional vinaigrette. Arrange the Citrus Confit around the salad if desired, alternating orange and grapefruit slices.

Serves six   *Wine Master's Suggestion*: Biltmore Limited Release Sauvignon Blanc

Citrus Confit

2 oranges
2 ruby red grapefruit
1/2 cup orange juice
2 tablespoons corn syrup
1 tablespoon minced fresh mint

Peel and section the oranges and grapefruit over a saucepan. Squeeze the remaining juice from the fruit into the saucepan and set the citrus sections aside. Stir in 1/2 cup orange juice and the corn syrup. Bring to a simmer over medium heat and cook until reduced by 3/4. Add the citrus sections and spoon into a bowl. Let stand until cool. Add the mint and mix gently. Store in the refrigerator.

Serves six

Herb-Roasted Chicken Salad with Frisée, Endive and Feta Cheese

Cabernet Vinaigrette
1/2 bottle Biltmore Cabernet Sauvignon
1/4 cup corn syrup
2 tablespoons red wine vinegar
2 teaspoons minced fresh thyme
1 teaspoon minced fresh rosemary
2/3 cup canola oil
salt and pepper to taste

Salad
1 head frisée
1 head Belgian endive
1 cup (4 ounces) crumbled feta cheese
1 cup chopped Herb-Roasted Chicken
  (below)
sliced Herb-Roasted Chicken breasts
  (below)

For the vinaigrette, simmer the wine in a saucepan until reduced to 1/4 cup. Stir in the corn syrup and let stand until cool. Whisk in the vinegar, thyme and rosemary. Add the canola oil gradually, whisking constantly to incorporate well. Season with salt and pepper.

For the salad, trim the bottoms from the frisée and endive. Separate the endive leaves and combine with the frisée in a bowl. Add half the vinaigrette and toss to coat evenly. Add the feta cheese and chopped Herb-Roasted Chicken. Spoon onto serving plates and arrange the Herb-Roasted Chicken breasts on the plates. Drizzle with the remaining vinaigrette.

Serves four   *Wine Master's Suggestion*: Biltmore Chardonnay sur Lies

Herb-Roasted Chicken

2 tablespoons minced parsley
2 tablespoons minced chives
2 tablespoons minced fresh basil
2 tablespoons minced fresh thyme

1 tablespoon minced garlic
2 teaspoons kosher salt
2 teaspoons freshly cracked pepper
1 (2- to 3-pound) whole young chicken

Preheat the oven to 350 degrees. Mix the parsley, chives, basil, thyme, garlic, kosher salt and pepper in a bowl. Lift the skin gently from the chicken breast area and insert the herb mixture under the skin. Place in a roasting pan and insert a meat thermometer into the thickest portion of the thigh. Roast for 45 to 60 minutes or to 160 degrees on the meat thermometer. Remove from the oven and let stand until cool. Remove the breast meat in whole pieces and cut into thick slices. Pull the remaining meat from the bones and chop. Reserve 1 cup of the chopped chicken for the salad and the remaining chopped chicken for another use.

Serves four   *Wine Master's Suggestion*: Biltmore Merlot

Mountain Trout with Almond Butter and Haricots Verts

The Biltmore prepares this dish with Red Mountain trout fillets from Sunburst Farms.

Haricots Verts
1 pound haricots verts
salt to taste
7 tablespoons butter
pepper to taste

Trout
4 (6- to 7-ounce) trout fillets
kosher salt and freshly ground
  white pepper to taste
1/4 cup olive oil
Almond Butter (below)

For the haricots verts, cut off the ends of the beans. Bring a large saucepan of water to a boil and add enough salt to taste like ocean water. Add the beans and cook for 4 minutes or until done to taste. Drain and plunge into ice water. Drain and place on paper towels to absorb the moisture.

Melt 4 tablespoons of the butter in a sauté pan. Add the beans and sauté for 2 minutes. Season with salt and pepper and add the remaining 3 tablespoons butter. Cook until any liquid has evaporated and the beans are glazed; keep warm.

For the trout, season the cut side of the fillets with kosher salt and white pepper. Heat a skillet over high heat and add the olive oil. Add the trout skin side down to the skillet and sear for 2 minutes; the skin will loosen from the pan as it sears. Give the pan a small shake to check if the skin is loosened and turn the fish with a fish spatula. Cook for 3 minutes longer and remove to hot plates. Add the beans to the plates. Spoon Almond Butter over the top.

Serves four

Wine Master's Suggestion: Biltmore Château Reserve Chardonnay

Almond Butter

1/2 cup blanched almonds
6 tablespoons butter, melted
juice of 2 lemons
2 tablespoons minced chives

Brown the almonds lightly in the butter in a sauté pan. Add the lemon juice and chives. Serve over fish.

Serves four

Shrimp-Stuffed Rigatoni in Chardonnay Thyme Sauce

Fresh bread or crostini is a wonderful accompaniment for this dish.

1/2 cup uncooked shrimp,
   peeled and deveined
2 garlic cloves, chopped
1 egg
2 tablespoons heavy cream
salt and pepper to taste
1 tablespoon chopped fresh thyme
14 rigatoni, cooked al dente and drained
Chardonnay Thyme Sauce (below)

1/4 cup (1/2 stick) butter, cut into cubes
juice of 1 lemon
1 teaspoon chopped fresh thyme
6 basil leaves

Garnish
3 ounces fresh crab meat
1 tomato, peeled, chopped and
   sautéed in butter

Combine the shrimp and garlic in a food processor and pulse for 1 minute. Add the egg and process until smooth. Add the cream gradually, processing to form a smooth paste. Season with salt and pepper. Spoon into a mixing bowl and stir in 1 tablespoon thyme.

Spoon half the shrimp mixture at a time into a piping bag fitted with a small round tip and pipe into the cooked rigatoni. Add the stuffed rigatoni to the Chardonnay Thyme Sauce and cook until the shrimp mixture is cooked through.

Discard the bay leaf and stir in the butter, lemon juice, 1 teaspoon thyme and the basil. Season with salt and pepper. Spoon onto serving plates and garnish with fresh crab meat and sautéed tomato.

Serves two   *Wine Master's Suggestion*: Biltmore Château Reserve Chardonnay

Chardonnay Thyme Sauce

2 garlic cloves, thinly sliced
1 shallot, thinly sliced
1 teaspoon olive oil
1/4 cup Biltmore Château Reserve Chardonnay
1 bay leaf
1/2 cup heavy cream

Sweat the garlic and shallot in the olive oil in a small saucepan over medium heat until tender. Add the wine, stirring to deglaze the saucepan. Add the bay leaf and cook until the mixture is reduced by 3/4. Add the cream and cook until reduced by 1/2. Keep warm until ready to use.

Serves two

Quail and Seafood Paella with Spring Vegetables

For this recipe, you will need to purchase fresh live mussels and clams from your seafood market. Any mussels or clams that do not close when tapped are no longer alive and should be discarded.

3 semi-boneless quail, cut into quarters
10 to 12 jumbo shrimp,
   peeled and deveined
salt and pepper to taste
2 tablespoons olive oil
2 fennel bulbs, chopped
1/2 cup quartered baby carrots

1/2 cup quartered baby turnips
1/2 cup quartered cherry tomatoes
1 cup green peas
8 ounces black mussels, rinsed
8 ounces clams, rinsed
Paella Rice (below)

Season the quail and shrimp with salt and pepper and grill or pan-grill until cooked through.
Heat the olive oil in a skillet and add the fennel. Sauté until caramelized. Add the carrots, turnips, tomatoes, peas, mussels and clams. Sauté until the clams and mussels open. Serve with the quail and shrimp over Paella Rice.

Serves four to six

Wine Master's Suggestion: Biltmore Pinot Noir

Paella Rice

2 tablespoons smoked bacon, chopped
3 tablespoons sliced blanched chorizo
6 garlic cloves, minced
3 or 4 shallots, thinly sliced
pinch of saffron
2 cups uncooked jasmine or basmati rice
1 to 2 tablespoons tomato paste
1/2 cup Biltmore Sauvignon Blanc

2 cups clam stock, heated
2 cups chicken broth, heated
4 thyme sprigs
salt and pepper to taste
2 tablespoons chopped Italian parsley
6 tablespoons butter
1/4 cup olive oil

Heat a heavy saucepan over medium heat. Cook the bacon in the saucepan until the drippings are rendered. Add the chorizo, garlic, shallots and saffron. Sauté for 2 to 3 minutes. Add the rice and sauté until coated well. Stir in the tomato paste and wine and cook for 4 minutes, stirring constantly. Stir in the clam stock and chicken broth.
Tie the thyme sprigs with kitchen twine and add to the saucepan. Bring to a boil and cover. Cook over medium-low heat for 20 to 25 minutes or until the rice is tender. Remove the thyme and season with salt and pepper; add the parsley and butter. Drizzle with the olive oil and keep warm.

Serves four to six

Smoked Salmon Croque Monsieur

1 tablespoon chopped fresh dill weed
8 ounces cream cheese, softened
2 slices sourdough bread
4 ounces smoked salmon
8 slices Gruyère cheese
2 tablespoons butter

Mix the dill weed with the cream cheese in a small bowl. Spread over one side of each bread slice and place the smoked salmon and Gruyère cheese between the slices. Melt the butter in a sauté pan and add the sandwich. Cook until the bread is golden brown on each side and the salmon is warm. Cut into quarters to serve.

Serves one

Wine Master's Suggestion:
Biltmore Limited Release
Sauvignon Blanc

Pauline Dresser Merrill

Edith Vanderbilt's sister, Pauline Merrill, visited Biltmore in March of 1904. Pauline recalled taking breakfast in the Louis XVI Room where she slept, luncheon in the Breakfast Room, tea at five o'clock in the Tapestry Gallery, and full-dress dinner in the Banquet Hall at eight o'clock.

"The dinner table, in the center of the room, being too large for common use, a small cosy round table is drawn up before the central fire, & there we dine each night, with 2 footmen in knee breeches, gold garters, etc. to serve & look de style!"

Rack of Spring Lamb with Red Onion Marmalade

2 racks lamb, trimmed
salt and pepper to taste
1/4 cup olive oil
8 garlic cloves
2 tablespoons Dijon mustard

2 tablespoons whole grain mustard
1 teaspoon chopped fresh thyme
1 teaspoon chopped fresh rosemary
3/4 cup bread crumbs
Red Onion Marmalade (below)

Preheat the oven to 400 degrees. Season the lamb with salt and pepper. Sear in 1 tablespoon of the olive oil in a heated skillet over high heat or on a grill.

Place the garlic in a saucepan and drizzle with the remaining olive oil. Cook over medium heat until the garlic is tender; cool and mash with a knife. Combine with the Dijon mustard, whole grain mustard, thyme and rosemary in a small bowl; mix well. Brush over the lamb and coat it with the bread crumbs.

Place the lamb in a roasting pan and insert a meat thermometer into the thickest portion. Roast at 400 degrees until the meat thermometer registers rare. Reduce the oven temperature to 350 degrees and roast until done to taste.

Cut into chops and serve with Red Onion Marmalade.

Serves four   *Wine Master's Suggestion*: Biltmore Château Reserve Cabernet Sauvignon

Red Onion Marmalade

3 red onions, thinly sliced
2 tablespoons olive oil
3/4 cup sugar
1/3 cup red wine vinegar
1 1/2 cups Biltmore Château
    Reserve Cabernet Sauvignon
1 1/2 cups port
1 star anise
1 cinnamon stick

Preheat the oven to 325 degrees. Sweat the onions in the olive oil in a heavy ovenproof saucepan over high heat for 10 to 12 minutes or until translucent, stirring frequently. Stir in the sugar, vinegar, cabernet and port. Add the star anise and cinnamon stick. Bring to a simmer and cover with foil. Place in the oven and bake for 2 1/2 to 3 hours or until done to taste, stirring every 20 minutes. Remove the star anise and cinnamon stick. Store in the refrigerator.

Serves four

Roasted Fresh Asparagus with Hazelnut Butter

Although asparagus can usually be found year round, it marks the beginning of spring for many people. If asparagus is hard to find, green beans can be substituted as they also combine well with the hazelnuts.

1 pound green asparagus, trimmed and peeled
2 tablespoons olive oil
2 teaspoons lemon juice
1 teaspoon kosher salt
1 teaspoon pepper
3 tablespoons Hazelnut Butter (below)

Preheat the oven to 425 degrees. Toss the asparagus with the olive oil, lemon juice, kosher salt and pepper in a bowl, coating well. Spread on a baking sheet and roast for 10 minutes or until tender. Serve with the Hazelnut Butter.

Serves two to four   *Wine Master's Suggestion*: Biltmore Château Reserve Chardonnay

Hazelnut Butter

1/3 cup crushed toasted hazelnuts
1/2 cup (1 stick) butter, softened
1 tablespoon minced shallot
2 tablespoons chopped parsley
1/2 teaspoon grated lemon zest
2 teaspoons lemon juice
1 tablespoon Frangelico
1 tablespoon honey
1 teaspoon kosher salt
1 teaspoon pepper

Combine the hazelnuts with the butter, shallot, parsley and lemon zest in the bowl of a small tabletop mixer. Add the lemon juice, liqueur, honey, kosher salt and pepper. Beat at low speed with a paddle attachment until well mixed, scraping the side of the bowl occasionally.

Shape into a log about 1 inch in diameter on plastic wrap or baking parchment. Wrap and chill until firm. Cut into 1/4-inch slices to serve.

Makes three-fourths cup

Broccoli with Toasted Garlic Oil

This dish elevates broccoli to something ambrosial. The broccoli has a delicate crispness and the garlic, when toasted, has a sweet nutty flavor that is not at all overpowering. It is a great accompaniment for an entrée or as a salad.

8 cloves garlic, finely minced (about 3 tablespoons)
1/2 cup olive oil
4 broccoli crowns
2 quarts water
2 tablespoons salt

Sauté the garlic in the olive oil in a heavy saucepan over low heat until light golden brown; do not overcook, as it will become bitter. Let cool to room temperature.

Cut the florets from the broccoli crowns, leaving 1/2 inch of the stems; reserve the stems for another use. Cut the florets lengthwise into halves or quarters, depending on their size.

Bring the water to a full boil in a saucepan and add the salt. Add the broccoli and reduce the heat. Simmer for 1 1/2 minutes or until tender-crisp. Drain in a colander and place the broccoli stem side up on two baking sheets lined with paper towels. Let stand until cool; this will allow the broccoli to cool without losing the seasoning or becoming water-logged.

Combine the broccoli with the garlic in a bowl and toss gently. Serve at room temperature or reheat gently in a sauté pan to serve warm.

Serves eight

Crocus neapolitanus

Biltmore Estate currently farms approximately 2,000 acres of land, including 250 acres devoted to corn and grain, 75 acres of vineyards, 10 acres of vegetable gardens, and 5 acres of nursery. The remainder provides pasture and hay for cattle, sheep, and horses. Biltmore Estate developed its farm conservation plan with the Buncombe County Soil and Water Conservation District and the Natural Resources Conservation Service. Sound management practices include cattle walkways, field buffers, cattle watering systems, and contained pesticide storage and mixing facilities. Biltmore has received the French Broad River Friendly Farmer Award for its efforts in water quality enhancement.

Crisp Potato Pizza with Sweet Peppers, Goat Cheese and Olive Tapenade

The potato crust for this pizza can be used as the base for any toppings you choose. It is a light spring and summer dish.

1 large Idaho potato, about 12 ounces
1/2 teaspoon kosher salt
1/4 teaspoon pepper
3 tablespoons clarified butter
1 1/2 tablespoons Olive Tapenade (below)
1/3 cup julienned roasted red bell pepper
2 ounces goat cheese, crumbled

1 cup coarsely chopped arugula
1/2 roasted red bell pepper, julienned
1 teaspoon olive oil
1 teaspoon lemon juice
1/4 teaspoon kosher salt
1/4 teaspoon pepper

Julienne the potato into 1 1/2- to 2-inch strips with a mandoline set on thin julienne setting; press to remove excess water. Toss with 1/2 teaspoon kosher salt and 1/4 teaspoon pepper. Heat a 7 1/2-inch nonstick skillet over medium heat and add half the butter. Add the potato and press down to form a cake. Reduce the heat to medium-low and cook for 15 minutes or until the bottom is golden brown, pressing frequently to retain the shape. Invert carefully onto a small plate. Melt the remaining butter in the skillet and return the potato cake to the skillet browned side up. Cook for 15 minutes longer or until golden brown. Remove to paper towels to drain. Place on a serving plate. Spread with the Olive Tapenade and sprinkle with 1/3 cup julienned roasted red bell pepper.

Toss the goat cheese, arugula and 1/2 roasted red bell pepper, julienned, with the olive oil and lemon juice in a small bowl. Season with 1/4 teaspoon kosher salt and 1/4 teaspoon pepper. Sprinkle over the pizza. Cut into 4 pieces and serve immediately as an entrée or appetizer.

Serves one or two

Wine Master's Suggestion: Biltmore Sauvignon Blanc

Olive Tapenade

This accompaniment is great with grilled bread or served with fish.

1 cup pitted kalamata olives
1 large garlic clove
1 tablespoon pine nuts
1 tablespoon chopped roasted
   red bell pepper

1 tablespoon chopped parsley
2 anchovies
1 teaspoon olive oil
1 teaspoon lemon juice

Combine the olives, garlic, pine nuts, bell pepper, parsley and anchovies in a food processor. Add the olive oil and lemon juice. Process until the mixture is smooth but still retains some texture, scraping down the side of the bowl as necessary. Store, covered, in the refrigerator.

Makes one and one-half cups

May Day

In the early 1900s, children from Biltmore Parish Day School, established by George Vanderbilt in 1897, participated in a traditional English May Day celebration in nearby Biltmore Village, dancing around a glass pole shipped all the way from Europe by Mr. Vanderbilt. Later, guests enjoyed an open-air dinner. The refreshments in 1905 included thirty-five gallons of ice cream and twenty-five dozen macaroons. Sarah Drake, daughter of farm worker Leander Drake, recalled that the May Pole "was way up and it had lots of streamers . . . each one of us would get it and run around and make it stripey." Sarah first tasted ice cream in 1910, at the age of sixteen!

Buttermilk Biscuits

For Cheddar and Chive Biscuits using this recipe, add 1 cup shredded Cheddar cheese and 3 to 4 tablespoons finely chopped fresh chives to the mixture before adding the buttermilk.

4 3/4 cups (or more) self-rising flour
1 teaspoon salt
3/4 cup vegetable shortening
2 cups buttermilk

Preheat the oven to 375 degrees. Mix the flour and salt in a large mixing bowl. Cut in the shortening with a pastry blender or your hands until the mixture forms pea-size crumbs. Add the buttermilk and mix with a spatula just until combined; the dough will be very wet.

Spoon onto a work surface generously dusted with flour. Sprinkle with additional flour and knead for 5 minutes or until the dough is smooth, adding additional flour as needed. Roll the dough to the desired thickness; the thicker the dough, the larger the biscuit. Cut as desired and arrange with sides touching on a baking sheet. Bake for 20 to 30 minutes or until golden brown. Serve warm.

For Cinnamon Biscuits, add 2 tablespoons cinnamon to the flour mixture. Frost slightly cooled Cinnamon Biscuits with a cream cheese frosting.

Makes sixteen

Focaccia Farcita

1/2 cup olive oil
2 yellow onions, julienned
4 teaspoons dry yeast
1 teaspoon sugar
5 1/2 cups bread flour
2 cups warm water
1 tablespoon dried oregano
1 tablespoon dried thyme
1 tablespoon dried basil
1 teaspoon salt

Heat a large skillet over medium-high heat and pour in 1 teaspoon of the olive oil. Add the onions and cook until the onions are caramelized.

Sprinkle the yeast, sugar and 1 tablespoon of the flour over the warm water in a small bowl. Stir to dissolve and let stand for 15 minutes or until the yeast is foamy. Mix the oregano, thyme and basil in a small bowl.

Combine 1 cup of the remaining flour, half the dried herbs and the salt in a mixing bowl and mix with the paddle attachment. Add the yeast mixture and mix at low speed. Add 2 tablespoons of the remaining olive oil and beat for 2 minutes. Add the remaining flour 1/2 cup at a time, mixing well after each addition. Add the caramelized onions and mix to form a dough that just clears the side of the bowl, adding additional water if needed.

Replace the paddle attachment with the dough hook and knead the dough for 2 to 3 minutes or until smooth and elastic; the dough should not spring back when pressed with your finger. Place in a lightly oiled bowl, turning to coat evenly. Cover with plastic wrap and let rise at room temperature for 1 1/2 hours or until tripled in bulk.

Grease an 11×17-inch baking sheet and sprinkle with cornmeal. Place the dough on a lightly floured work surface and press with the heel of your hand to flatten. Lift and pull the dough gently, transferring it to the baking sheet and stretching to cover the pan. Cover with plastic wrap and let rise for 30 to 60 minutes or until doubled in bulk. Mix the remaining dried herbs with the remaining olive oil in a small bowl; let stand while the dough is rising.

Preheat the oven to 400 degrees. Place a baking stone on the bottom oven rack for the best results. Press 1/4-inch indentations in the dough with your fingertips or knuckles. Drizzle the herbed olive oil over the dough or brush it on with a pastry brush; the oil can be allowed to puddle in the indentations. Place the dough directly on the heated stone or oven rack. Bake for 35 to 40 minutes or until golden brown. Cool slightly on a wire rack and serve warm plain or sprinkled with coarse salt.

Makes one 11×17-inch focaccia

Blueberry French Toast

2 cups milk
4 eggs
2 tablespoons sugar, or to taste
ground cinnamon and nutmeg to taste
salt to taste
butter for frying
1 loaf Blueberry Brioche Bread, sliced
  (below)

Combine the milk, eggs, sugar, cinnamon, nutmeg and salt in a bowl and whisk until smooth. Store in the refrigerator until needed. Heat a skillet and add butter or spray with nonstick cooking spray. Dip the bread slices into the egg mixture a few at a time and place in the skillet. Fry until evenly brown on both sides. Serve immediately.

Serves six to eight

Blueberry Brioche Bread

4 envelopes (4 tablespoons) dry yeast
3 cups milk
8 cups (2 pounds) bread flour
2 eggs
5 tablespoons butter, cut into cubes
nutmeg to taste
2 tablespoons sugar
1 teaspoon salt
2 pints fresh blueberries

Dissolve the yeast in the milk in a mixing bowl. Add half the flour and mix well. Let stand in a warm place for 15 minutes. Add the eggs, butter and nutmeg and mix well at low speed with a dough hook. Add the remaining flour, sugar, salt and blueberries. Mix at low speed until the mixture begins to come together, scraping the side of the bowl occasionally. Increase the speed to medium and mix until the dough is smooth and elastic when pressed.

Remove to a lightly oiled bowl and turn to coat the surface. Cover with plastic wrap and let rise at room temperature for 20 minutes or until doubled in bulk; the dough should retain an indentation when pressed. Punch down the dough and fold it over to remove any air pockets and redistribute the yeast.

Preheat the oven to 350 degrees. Remove the dough to a floured work surface and cut into 4 pieces. Place in greased loaf pans and bake for 25 to 30 minutes or until golden brown on the top. Remove to a wire rack to cool completely. Cut into slices when cool.

Makes four loaves

Raspberry Cream Cheese Coffee Cake

1/4 cup packed brown sugar
1 cup finely ground pecans
2 teaspoons cinnamon
2 cups all-purpose flour
1 1/2 teaspoons baking powder
1 teaspoon baking soda
1/2 cup (1 stick) butter, softened
1 cup granulated sugar
2 eggs
1 cup sour cream
2 teaspoons vanilla extract
1 teaspoon cinnamon
1/4 cup pecan halves
1 1/2 cups fresh raspberries

Garnish
confectioners' sugar, toasted pecans and/or
    additional raspberries

Preheat the oven to 320 degrees. Mix the brown sugar, ground pecans and 2 teaspoons cinnamon in a small bowl and set aside.

Sift the flour, baking powder and baking soda into a medium bowl. Cream the butter and sugar in a mixing bowl until light and fluffy. Beat in the eggs and then the sour cream until smooth. Add the sifted ingredients gradually, beating constantly and scraping the side of the bowl occasionally. Stir in the vanilla and 1 teaspoon cinnamon.

Sprinkle the pecan halves over the bottom of a buttered and floured 10- to 12-inch bundt pan. Sprinkle 1/4 cup of the ground pecan mixture evenly over the pecan halves. Stir the remaining ground pecan mixture into the coffee cake batter. Fold in the raspberries. Spoon the batter into the prepared pan and spread evenly.

Bake for 30 to 40 minutes or until a wooden pick inserted into the center comes out clean. Cool in the pan for 20 minutes and invert onto a plate. Garnish with confectioners' sugar, toasted pecans and/or fresh raspberries.

Serves twelve

Wine Master's Suggestion:
Biltmore Methode Champenoise Pas de Deux Sec

Citrus and Goat Cheese Panna Cotta

Grapefruit Gelée
2 gelatin sheets, or 2 tablespoons unflavored gelatin
3/4 cup grapefruit juice
1/4 cup sugar

Panna Cotta
7 gelatin sheets, or 7 tablespoons unflavored gelatin
3 cups heavy cream
6 tablespoons sugar
14 ounces goat cheese, softened

For the gelée, place the gelatin sheets in cold water and let stand to absorb the water. Combine the grapefruit juice and sugar in a small saucepan and bring to a boil. Reduce to a simmer and add the gelatin sheets, whisking to dissolve completely. Pour evenly into six 4-ounce glasses or ramekins. Chill until firm.

For the panna cotta, soften the gelatin sheets as directed for the gelée. Bring the cream and sugar to a boil in a medium saucepan and remove from the heat. Add the gelatin and whisk to dissolve completely. Whisk in the goat cheese. Spoon evenly into the prepared ramekins.

Run a knife around the side of the ramekins to loosen the panna cotta and invert onto serving plates or serve in the glasses or ramekins with fresh grapefruit.

Serves six

Wine Master's Suggestion:
Biltmore Sauvignon Blanc

Etiquette dictated carefully planned seating for formal dinners. Honored guests always sat to the right of the host and hostess, and husbands and wives were separated with unmarried diners mixed in-between, to balance guests' statuses and promote stimulating conversation. Edith Vanderbilt kept a small notebook in which she recorded seating arrangements for Banquet Hall dinners. Early diagrams show that she and Mr. Vanderbilt originally sat at opposite ends of the table, but by 1900 they sat in the center to be more accessible. The largest party, for thirty-six guests, took place in April of 1908 to honor Lord Grey, Governor General of Canada.

Coconut Cake

3/4 cup (1 1/2 sticks) butter, softened
1 2/3 cups sugar
3 eggs
1 1/2 cups sour cream
1 3/4 cups self-rising flour
1/2 cup milk

1 tablespoon coconut extract
1 1/4 cups coconut, toasted and cooled
Creamy Frosting (below)

Garnish
additional toasted coconut

Preheat the oven to 350 degrees. Cream the butter and sugar in a mixing bowl until light and fluffy. Beat in the eggs. Add the sour cream and mix well. Add the flour alternately with the milk, mixing well after each addition. Mix in the coconut extract and then the toasted coconut. Spread the batter in a deep round cake pan. Bake for 50 to 60 minutes or until the cake tests done. Cool in the pan for several minutes and remove to a wire rack to cool completely. Chill in the refrigerator. Trim off the top of the chilled cake to make it level and cut the cake carefully into 3 layers with a large bread knife.

Spread Creamy Frosting between the layers and over the top and side of the cake. Garnish with additional toasted coconut.

You may bake the cake in 3 layers if preferred, adjusting the baking time accordingly.

Serves twelve   *Wine Master's Suggestion*: Biltmore Methode Champenoise Pas de Deux Sec

Creamy Frosting

3/4 cup (1 1/2 sticks) butter, softened
1/2 cup shortening
6 ounces cream cheese, softened
1 (1-pound) package confectioners' sugar
1 tablespoon water

Cream the butter, shortening and cream cheese in a mixing bowl until light. Sift in the confectioners' sugar and mix until fluffy. Add the water and beat until smooth.

Fills and frosts one cake

Hazelnut Cake

1 1/2 cups cake flour
1/2 teaspoon baking soda
1/2 teaspoon salt
3/4 cup (1 1/2 sticks) butter, softened
1 1/2 cups sugar
4 egg yolks
1/2 cup sour cream
3/4 cup (6 ounces) hazelnuts, toasted and
    finely ground

4 egg whites
1/4 teaspoon salt
1 (12-ounce) jar raspberry jam
Butter Frosting (below)

Garnish
toasted whole hazelnuts

Preheat the oven to 350 degrees. Sift the flour, baking soda and 1/2 teaspoon salt together. Cream the butter and sugar in a mixing bowl until light and fluffy. Beat in the egg yolks. Add the sifted ingredients alternately with the sour cream in 3 additions, mixing well after each addition. Mix in the hazelnuts.

Beat the egg whites in a mixing bowl until frothy. Add 1/4 teaspoon salt and beat until soft peaks form. Fold into the batter with a spatula. Spoon into a greased and floured deep round cake pan.

Bake the cake for 50 to 60 minutes or until a knife or wooden pick inserted into the center comes out clean. Cool in the pan for several minutes and invert onto a wire rack to cool completely. Chill in the refrigerator. Trim off the top of the chilled cake to make it level and cut the cake carefully into 3 layers with a large bread knife. Spread 3/4 of the raspberry jam between the layers. Chill in the refrigerator. Spread the Butter Frosting over the top and side of the cake. Chill until the frosting is firm. Spread the remaining raspberry jam over the top of the frosted cake. Garnish with toasted whole hazelnuts.

You may bake the cake in 3 layers if preferred, adjusting the baking time accordingly.

Serves twelve   *Wine Master's Suggestion*: Biltmore Methode Champenoise Sparkling Sec

Butter Frosting

3/4 cup (1 1/2 sticks) butter, softened
1/2 cup shortening
1 (1-pound) package confectioners' sugar
1 tablespoon water

Cream the butter and shortening in a mixing bowl until light. Sift in the confectioners' sugar and beat until fluffy. Add the water and beat until smooth.

Frosts one cake

Red Velvet Cake with Cream Cheese Frosting

Although there is much debate as to the origins of this very colorful cake, no one can deny its popularity and presence on the southern table. Our version is layered with rich cream cheese frosting and is "velvety" enough to tempt anyone's taste buds.

4 1/2 cups cake flour
2 teaspoons baking soda
2 teaspoons baking cocoa
3 cups sugar
2 3/4 cups vegetable oil
5 eggs, lightly beaten

1 3/4 cups buttermilk
4 teaspoons vinegar
2 teaspoons vanilla extract
1/4 cup red food coloring
Cream Cheese Frosting (below)

Preheat the oven to 300 degrees. Sift the flour, baking soda and baking cocoa together. Combine the sugar, oil and eggs in a mixing bowl and beat at medium speed with a paddle attachment until smooth. Add the sifted ingredients gradually, mixing well. Add the buttermilk, vinegar, vanilla and food coloring, mixing just until combined.

Spray a deep 10-inch cake pan with nonstick cooking spray and line the bottom with a circle of baking parchment. Spread the cake batter in the prepared pan. Bake for 40 to 50 minutes or until a wooden pick inserted into the center comes out clean. Cool in the pan for 10 minutes and remove to a wire rack to cool completely. Trim off the top of the cake to make it level and cut the cake carefully into 3 layers with a large bread knife; reserve the trimmings for a crumb garnish. Spread Cream Cheese Frosting between the layers and over the top and side of the cake.

You may bake the cake in 3 layers if preferred, adjusting the baking time accordingly.

Serves twelve   *Wine Master's Suggestion*: Biltmore Winemaker's Selection Chenin Blanc

Cream Cheese Frosting

3/4 cup (1 1/2 sticks) butter, softened
12 ounces cream cheese, softened
2/3 cup shortening
2 (1-pound) packages confectioners' sugar

Combine the butter, cream cheese and shortening in a mixing bowl. Beat at medium speed with a paddle attachment until light, scraping the side of the bowl occasionally. Add the confectioners' sugar gradually and beat for 5 minutes or until fluffy.

Fills and frosts one cake

Southern-Style Chocolate Chess Pie

This version of the southern classic has a fudgy texture.

1 unbaked (9-inch) frozen pie shell
1/2 cup (1 stick) unsalted butter
1/4 cup chopped unsweetened chocolate
1 cup sugar
2 eggs
1 tablespoon bourbon
1 teaspoon vanilla extract
1/4 teaspoon salt
1 cup pecans (optional)

Garnish
whipped cream

Preheat the oven to 325 degrees. Bake the pie shell for 10 minutes. Cool on a wire rack. Place a baking sheet in the oven.

Combine the butter and chocolate in a small heavy saucepan. Cook over medium heat until melted, stirring until smooth. Cool for 10 minutes.

Whisk the sugar and eggs together in a medium bowl. Whisk in the chocolate mixture, bourbon, vanilla and salt. Stir in the pecans; the filling will be thick. Spoon into the prepared pie shell.

Place on the baking sheet in the oven and bake for 30 minutes or until the center is set and the edges of the filling puff and begin to crack. Cool on a wire rack. Garnish with whipped cream.

Serves six to eight

Wine Master's Suggestion: Biltmore Century

Lavender Martini

ice
1 ounce (2 tablespoons) gin
1¹/2 teaspoons Triple Sec
1¹/2 teaspoons Campari
1¹/2 teaspoons simple syrup
2 teaspoons lemon juice

Garnish
1 fresh lavender sprig

Fill a cocktail shaker with ice. Add the gin, Triple Sec, Campari, simple syrup and lemon juice. Shake well and strain into a chilled martini glass. Garnish with the lavender sprig.

Serves one

Poma amoris fructu rubro.

Asheville was the mountain

resort of choice at the turn

of the nineteenth century during

the hot, humid months

that blanketed much of the South.

The Blue Ridge Mountains

offered a mild summer breeze and

a cool escape from the heat.

Summer

Summer

horseback riding, camping, fishing, picnicking, and carriage outings. Friends and family visiting from New York and Newport came to Biltmore Estate to relax and escape the hustle and bustle of daily life. They found themselves rejuvenated by the fresh air and exercise. And, undoubtedly, they also found

Asheville was the mountain resort of choice at the turn of the nineteenth century during the hot, humid months that blanketed much of the South. The Blue Ridge Mountains offered a mild summer breeze and a cool escape from the heat. The Vanderbilts took advantage of the beauty of the region and the plethora of outdoor activities the estate offered—hiking,

themselves happily hungry after a day of activities. Fortunately, Biltmore's farms and gardens overflowed

throughout the summertime with fresh vegetables and fruits, dairy products, lamb, poultry, and eggs.

Kitchen staff at Biltmore House were charged with canning, pickling, curing, and preserving so that the

pantries were well stocked for fall and winter. The kitchens also hummed with spontaneity as guests

embarked on impromptu outings requiring a hamper of fresh food and drink. Guests could take in the last

summer's evening on the Loggia or Library Terrace overlooking the French Broad Valley before retiring

to their rooms upstairs, where they were lulled to sleep by the soft wind from the valleys, the sound of

cicadas, the glow of lightning bugs on the night air, and the smell of honeysuckle and summer rain.

Summer Grilling Menu

Watermelon Gazpacho

Coleslaw

Grilled Marinated Flank Steak with
Mango and Black Bean Salsa

Carolina Pulled Pork

Barbecued Spareribs

Strawberry Pie

Banana Slush Punch

Barbecued Spareribs

Goat Cheese and Risotto Fritters with Tomato Jam

3 cups chicken stock or chicken broth
1/4 cup (1/2 stick) butter
1 yellow onion, minced
2 garlic cloves, minced
1 cup uncooked arborio rice
1/2 cup (2 ounces) grated Parmesan cheese
1 cup crumbled goat cheese
1/4 cup (1/2 stick) butter
2 tablespoons kosher salt
2 teaspoons white pepper
2 tablespoons chopped fresh basil

2 tablespoons chopped fresh oregano
1/4 cup chopped fresh parsley
2 cups all-purpose flour
3 eggs, lightly beaten
2 cups bread crumbs
vegetable oil for deep-frying
Tomato Jam (below)

Garnish
chopped basil and parsley

Heat the chicken stock in a saucepan and maintain at a low simmer. Melt 1/4 cup butter in a heavy stockpot and heat until frothy. Add the onion and garlic and sauté until translucent but not brown. Add the rice and sauté for 1 minute, stirring to coat with butter.

Add the heated chicken stock 1/3 at a time and cook until the liquid is absorbed after each addition, stirring with a wooden spoon so as not to break up the rice; the total cooking time will be about 20 minutes.

Remove from the heat and add the Parmesan cheese, goat cheese, 1/4 cup butter, the kosher salt and white pepper. Stir in the basil, oregano and parsley. Spread on a baking sheet and chill in the refrigerator.

Scoop the risotto into rounded balls. Dip the balls into the flour, then into the eggs and coat with the bread crumbs. Chill or freeze until serving time.

Preheat oil to 350 degrees in a deep fryer. Add the fritters in batches and deep-fry until golden brown. Serve in a small bowl with Tomato Jam and garnish with additional chopped basil and parsley.

Makes twenty-four

Wine Master's Suggestion: Biltmore Pinot Grigio

Tomato Jam

3 slicing tomatoes
1/4 cup olive oil
2 cups apple cider
2 tablespoons sugar

1 tablespoon pectin
1 cinnamon stick
4 whole cloves
1 tablespoon kosher salt

Preheat the oven to 350 degrees. Brush the whole tomatoes with the olive oil and place in a roasting pan. Roast for 10 to 15 minutes or until the skins begin to peel. Cool to room temperature. Remove and discard the skins and stems. Cut the tomatoes into halves, discarding the seeds and excess juice. Chop into medium pieces.

Combine the tomatoes with the apple cider, sugar, pectin, cinnamon stick, whole cloves and kosher salt in a saucepan. Bring to a boil and reduce the heat. Simmer for 45 to 60 minutes or until a syrupy consistency. Remove the cinnamon stick and whole cloves. Spoon into an airtight container and store in the refrigerator.

Serves four to six

Carolina Crab Cakes

Crab cakes can be prepared in advance for convenience. After browning, store them on a baking parchment-lined tray and refrigerate them until time to bake.

> 2 pounds pasteurized jumbo lump crab meat
> 2 eggs
> 1/4 cup Japanese-style bread crumbs, or as needed to bind the crab cakes
> 2 tablespoons minced chives
> juice of 1/2 lemon
> 1/3 cup mayonnaise
> 11/2 tablespoons Dijon mustard
> 11/2 tablespoons whole grain mustard
> 1 tablespoon Old Bay seasoning
> salt and pepper to taste
> 2 tablespoons mild olive oil or butter

Preheat the oven to 325 degrees. Pick through the crab meat to remove any bits of shell. Combine with the eggs, bread crumbs and chives in a medium bowl. Add the lemon juice, mayonnaise, Dijon mustard, whole grain mustard, Old Bay seasoning, salt and pepper; mix well with a wooden spoon or gloved hands. Shape tightly into balls and flatten gently to form cakes, placing on a baking parchment-lined pan sprinkled with additional bread crumbs.

Heat a medium skillet over medium heat and add the olive oil. Add the crab cakes in batches of 4 or 5 and cook until golden brown on the bottom. Turn the cakes and cook for 1 minute longer. Remove to a baking pan lined with baking parchment or sprayed with nonstick cooking spray. Bake for 15 minutes or until cooked through. Serve immediately.

Makes six to eight crab cakes

Wine Master's Suggestion:
Biltmore Sauvignon Blanc

The Kitchen Staff

The chef oversaw all kitchen activities. He supervised the cook and kitchen maids, ordered all food items, and maintained the kitchen pantries and equipment. He suggested the menus for the Vanderbilts' meals and prepared luncheons and dinners, while the cook prepared breakfast for the family and guests and all three meals for the domestic staff. Cook's assistants and kitchen maids prepared fruits, vegetables, and meats for cooking and kept the kitchens clean while food was being prepared, scrubbing copper pots and washing utensils. The pastry chef oversaw the creation of desserts for luncheons, teas, and dinners.

The Butler's Pantry

Two Otis Brothers & Co. dumbwaiters transported food from the Kitchen Pantry to the Butler's Pantry. In the Butler's Pantry, china and crystal were stored in built-in cabinets and washed in sinks beneath the window or in the adjacent pantry and butler's office at the end of the hall. The room also served as a central communication point for the Biltmore House domestic staff. A telephone, part of an in-house system, and speaking tubes allowed butlers to communicate with the chef. Mounted on the wall in the hallway outside is the main call box for the annunciator system that allowed family and guests to summon servants by pressing ivory buttons throughout the house.

Mango and Black Bean Salsa

This is especially good with the Grilled Marinated Flank Steak on page 72.

2 cups cooked black beans
1 mango, chopped
1 small red onion, chopped
1/2 green bell pepper, chopped
1/2 yellow bell pepper, chopped
1/2 red bell pepper, chopped
1 jalapeño chile, seeded and chopped
3 tablespoons chopped cilantro
1/4 teaspoon chili powder
1/4 teaspoon ground cumin
1/2 teaspoon kosher salt
1/4 teaspoon crushed red pepper
1/2 teaspoon ground black pepper
1 tablespoon fresh lime juice
3 tablespoons olive oil

Combine the black beans, mango, onion, bell peppers and jalapeño chile in a bowl. Add the cilantro, chili powder, cumin, kosher salt, red pepper and black pepper; mix well. Stir in the lime juice and olive oil. Serve with chips or as an accompaniment for fish, chicken or beef.

Makes four cups

Chorizo-Stuffed Tomatoes

You can serve this summer specialty as a side dish or an appetizer. Prepare them in advance and bake at serving time.

4 whole slicing tomatoes
2 links chorizo, casings removed
3 slices bacon, chopped
1 yellow onion, minced
2 ribs celery, minced
1 carrot, minced
1 garlic clove, minced
4 button mushrooms, sliced

4 shiitake mushrooms, sliced
salt to taste
butter or olive oil for sautéing
1 cup crumbled Corn Bread (below)
2 tablespoons chopped fresh sage
1/4 cup chopped fresh parsley
1/2 cup (1 stick) butter, cut into small cubes

Remove the stems from the tomatoes and cut a small X on the bottoms. Place in a saucepan of boiling water for 1 minute or until the skins can be easily slipped off. Plunge into ice water to cool and discard the skins. Cut the tomatoes into halves, discarding the seeds.

Crumble the sausage. Cook with the bacon in a heated sauté pan, stirring to brown evenly. Remove the sausage and bacon to a bowl, reserving the drippings in the sauté pan.

Add the onion, celery, carrot and garlic to the reserved drippings and sauté until tender. Add the button mushrooms and shiitake mushrooms and sprinkle with salt. Sauté for 5 minutes or until the excess moisture evaporates, adding a small amount of butter or oil if needed. Add the vegetables to the sausage mixture and mix well. Stir in the corn bread, sage, parsley and 1/2 cup butter. Let stand until cool.

Preheat the oven to 350 degrees. Spoon the sausage mixture into the tomato halves and place in a baking pan. Bake for 15 minutes or until heated through.

Serves four

Corn Bread

2 cups cornmeal
2 cups all-purpose flour
1 tablespoon baking powder
1 teaspoon baking soda
1 teaspoon salt
4 eggs
1 cup sugar
1 cup buttermilk
1/2 cup (1 stick) butter, melted

Preheat the oven to 400 degrees. Sift the cornmeal, flour, baking powder, baking soda and salt into a bowl. Add the eggs, sugar, buttermilk and butter and mix well. Spoon into a 9×13-inch nonstick baking pan. Bake for 25 minutes.

Serves twelve

Citrus Ceviche of Bass

2 pounds sea bass, corvina or grouper, finely chopped
1 1/2 tablespoons salt
3 ribs celery, finely chopped
5 Roma tomatoes, finely chopped
1 red onion, finely chopped
1 bunch green onions, finely chopped
2 jalapeño chiles, seeded and minced
1 red bell pepper, finely chopped
1 bunch cilantro, chopped
1 1/2 tablespoons chopped peeled ginger
juice of 8 lemons
juice of 15 limes
juice of 5 oranges
1/4 cup rice wine vinegar
3 tablespoons tequila

Season the sea bass with the salt in a nonreactive bowl and place in the refrigerator for 5 to 6 hours. Press the bass to extract as much liquid as possible. Combine with the celery, tomatoes, red onion, green onions, jalapeño chiles, bell pepper, cilantro and ginger in a large bowl. Add the lemon juice, lime juice, orange juice, vinegar and tequila and mix gently. Chill for 3 to 5 hours before serving. Serve with crackers or toasted bread.

Serves four to six

Wine Master's Suggestion:
Biltmore Methode Champenoise Blanc de Blanc Brut

Cornelia's Bass

The Vanderbilts and their guests often fished in the French Broad River as well as in the Lagoon and Bass Pond on Biltmore Estate. Edith Vanderbilt is seen fishing in several archival images, and she passed on her love of the sport to her daughter. The fish served for dinner on Thursday, October 27, 1904, was a bass that four-year-old Cornelia had caught the day before. Four years later, a July New York Times article noted that Mrs. Vanderbilt had given a fishing party on the estate and landed twenty large mountain trout, the largest catch of the day.

This photograph is of Edith and Cornelia Vanderbilt and two unidentified guests fishing in the Lagoon in 1906.

Biltmore Bacon and Eggs

The cook was in no danger of running out of ingredients when Mr. Vanderbilt requested shirred (baked) eggs and bacon. An 1896 memorandum addressing complaints that Biltmore House was not receiving its due share of eggs noted that 115 dozen eggs had been sent over from the Poultry Farm the previous month, equal to nearly 30 dozen a week! The document also noted that the house had received 183 pounds of butter during the same period. Bacon from Biltmore's purebred Berkshire hogs was cured in the smokehouse after it left the estate butcher's shop on its way to Mr. Vanderbilt's breakfast tray.

Champagne Peach Bisque

Serve this cold soup when the weather is hot for a great summertime snack, for lunch, or for a dinner course. You can substitute Cointreau or Grand Marnier for the peach schnapps if you prefer.

3 cups sliced peeled fresh peaches
1 1/2 cups sour cream
1/2 cup milk
1 cup Biltmore Methode Champenoise
   Sparkling Sec
1 teaspoon peach schnapps
1 tablespoon lemon juice
3/4 cup sugar
1 tablespoon vanilla extract

Garnish
sliced peaches
fresh mint leaves

Combine the peaches, sour cream, milk, wine, schnapps, lemon juice, sugar and vanilla in a food processor or blender; process until smooth. Remove to a bowl and chill in the refrigerator. Ladle into small soup bowls and garnish with additional sliced peaches and a mint leaf.

Serves six to eight

Chilled Yellow Tomato Soup

1 pound yellow onions, chopped
2 fennel bulbs, chopped
1/2 cup chopped garlic
1 cup (2 sticks) butter, melted
1 cup marsala wine
4 pounds yellow tomatoes, peeled
   and chopped
1 pound yellow bell peppers, roasted

1/2 gallon chicken stock
2 tablespoons honey
salt to taste
1 teaspoon crushed red pepper
1 1/2 teaspoons ground white pepper
2 cups olive oil
Sweet Tomato Marmalade (below)
Lemon Mascarpone (below)

Sweat the onions, fennel and garlic in the butter in a large stockpot until tender. Add the wine, stirring to deglaze. Cook until the liquid evaporates. Add the tomatoes and bell peppers and cook for 10 minutes. Stir in the chicken stock and bring to a simmer over medium heat. Add the honey, salt, crushed red pepper and white pepper and mix well. Add the olive oil gradually, processing with an immersion blender until puréed. Adjust the seasonings and ladle into soup bowls. Top each serving with a dollop of Sweet Tomato Marmalade and Lemon Mascarpone.

Serves four to six

Wine Master's Suggestion: Biltmore Viognier

Sweet Tomato Marmalade and Lemon Mascarpone

Sweet Tomato Marmalade
4 slicing tomatoes
1/2 cup sugar
1 teaspoon salt
grated zest and juice of 2 lemons

Lemon Mascarpone
2 cups (8 ounces) mascarpone cheese
grated zest and juice of 1 lemon
1 tablespoon honey
salt and white pepper to taste

For the marmalade, heat the tomatoes with a kitchen torch until the skins blister; remove the skins. Cut the tomatoes into halves and squeeze out the seeds and excess juice. Chop into medium pieces and combine with the sugar and salt in a saucepan. Cook over medium heat until the liquid is syrupy and the tomatoes are tender. Stir in the lemon zest and lemon juice. Store in an airtight container in the refrigerator until needed.

For the lemon mascarpone, combine the mascarpone cheese with the lemon zest, lemon juice, honey, salt and white pepper in a bowl and mix well. Store in the refrigerator until needed.

Serves four to six

Watermelon Gazpacho

4 cups chopped seeded watermelon
1/4 cup chopped red bell pepper
1/4 cup chopped red onion
1 cup chopped seeded cucumber
2 tablespoons chopped seeded green chiles
2 large tomatoes, chopped
1/4 cup sliced scallions
4 garlic cloves, chopped
2 tablespoons chopped fresh cilantro
juice of 3 limes
salt and freshly ground white pepper to taste

Combine the watermelon, bell pepper, onion, cucumber, green chiles, tomatoes, scallions, garlic and cilantro in a large bowl. Add the lime juice, salt and white pepper and toss to mix well. Marinate in the refrigerator for 2 to 3 hours. Process in a blender or with an immersion blender until smooth. Adjust the seasonings and chill until serving time. Ladle into soup bowls to serve.

Serves four to six

Wine Master's Suggestion:
Biltmore Century

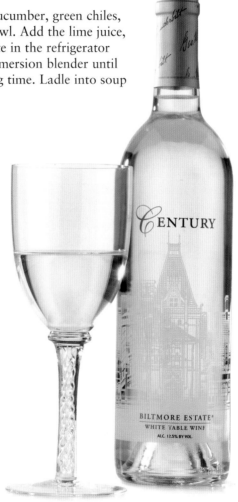

Cornelia's Birthday Parties

Cornelia's August birthday parties often took place in the Biltmore House Banquet Hall. One held in the early 1900s featured a cake with baked-in metal charms meant to predict the futures of the children who discovered them. The one who found a hidden dime would grow up to be rich. Mrs. Vanderbilt became alarmed, however, when no one found the dime that year. Fearing that someone had swallowed it, she frantically cut into the cake in search of it. Mildred Vanderhoof, who attended the party, thought it funny that someone so rich should worry about losing a dime!

For Cornelia's 25th birthday in 1925, estate employees presented her with a Biltmore Dairy cake made with 26 gallons of Lady Ashe ice cream, chocolate parfait, and vanilla mousse. Studded with roses and lilies, the two-by-four confection was inscribed, "May your joys be as many as the sands in the sea." Cornelia also celebrated with an open air ball for three hundred guests, who danced to the Charles Freicher Orchestra in a garden pavilion. Japanese lanterns hung from trees and shrubbery. One newspaper article noted that the ladies were as "beautiful as . . . fireflies in a fairy garden." Guests enjoyed a buffet supper at midnight.

Shrimp and Corn Chowder

This delicious soup is the kind that most people have in mind when they think of comfort food.

2 cups chopped yellow onions
8 garlic cloves, minced
8 ounces bacon, finely chopped
2 tablespoons olive oil
1 cup all-purpose flour
1 quart (4 cups) chicken stock
1 quart (4 cups) heavy cream

1 tablespoon salt
1/4 teaspoon white pepper
1 cup finely chopped carrots
2 cups frozen corn
2 tablespoons chopped fresh dill weed
2 pounds large shrimp, peeled, deveined
   and cut into thirds

Sauté the onions, garlic and bacon in the olive oil in a saucepan over medium heat until the onions are translucent and most of the drippings have been rendered from the bacon. Reduce the heat and stir in the flour. Cook for 1 minute, stirring constantly.

Mix in the chicken stock, cream, salt and white pepper and bring to a boil, stirring occasionally. Add the carrots, corn and dill weed and return to a boil. Stir in the shrimp and simmer over low heat for 5 minutes. Ladle into soup bowls and serve immediately.

Serves sixteen   *Wine Master's Suggestion*: Biltmore Château Methode Champenoise Brut

Coleslaw

This zesty slaw perfectly complements sandwiches, hamburgers, and hot dogs. It is also the essential ingredient in a Carolina barbecued pulled-pork sandwich.

Coleslaw Dressing
1 cup cider vinegar
1 cup sugar
1 teaspoon celery seeds
1/2 teaspoon dry mustard
1/2 teaspoon granulated garlic
1 teaspoon chili powder
1 teaspoon dried oregano

1 teaspoon salt
1/4 teaspoon cayenne pepper
3 cups mayonnaise

Coleslaw
6 cups shredded cabbage
1/2 cup shredded carrot

For the dressing, combine the vinegar, sugar, celery seeds, dry mustard, granulated garlic, chili powder, oregano, salt and cayenne pepper in a saucepan and mix well. Cook over medium heat until reduced by 1/2. Remove from the heat and let stand until cool.

Add the vinegar reduction gradually to the mayonnaise in a food processor, pulsing to incorporate well. Store in the refrigerator for up to two weeks.

For the slaw, combine the cabbage and carrot in a bowl and add the dressing; mix well. Store in the refrigerator until time to serve.

Serves six to eight

Bibb Lettuce Salad with Buttermilk Dill Dressing

Buttermilk Dill Dressing
1/4 cup buttermilk
1 cup mayonnaise
1/2 cup honey
1/4 cup sour cream
1/4 cup lemon juice
3 ounces fresh dill weed, chopped
kosher salt and ground pepper to taste

Salad
leaves of 3 small heads Bibb lettuce
1 cup cherry tomato halves
1 English cucumber, finely chopped
1/4 cup crumbled crisp-fried bacon
1/2 cup crumbled gorgonzola cheese

For the dressing, combine the buttermilk, mayonnaise, honey, sour cream, lemon juice, dill weed, kosher salt and pepper in a bowl and mix well.

For the salad, place the lettuce in the centers of chilled salad plates. Add the cherry tomatoes, cucumber, bacon and gorgonzola cheese. Drizzle the dressing around the lettuce.

Serves four to six

Family Gardens

Nearly every family living on Biltmore Estate cultivated a garden. Many also kept chickens and hogs. The Redmons, who ran a dairy on the West Side, always had a big garden, and the children were expected to help tend it. They grew green peas, Irish and sweet potatoes, okra, peppers, beans, and tomatoes and had canned green beans at most dinners and suppers. Even so, Edith Vanderbilt was concerned with the lack of variety in the diets of families living on the estate, so she offered a prize to the gardener who grew the greatest variety of vegetables and fruits.

This photograph, taken c. 1897, is of Lillie Souther Young and her daughter. It was donated by Alice Huskins.

Menu Planning

Biltmore's chef created the menus for meals served to the Vanderbilts and their guests, writing them in a ledger that was filled and replaced seasonally. He gave the ledger to the head housekeeper, who met daily with Mrs. Vanderbilt in the Oak Sitting Room to review menus and plan for the day's meals. The housekeeper next met with the chef and head butler to review the plans. She also ensured that appropriate table linens were delivered from the linen closet to the dining rooms and returned the linens to the laundry to be washed and ironed.

Grilled Salmon Salad

This is a wonderful light salad for a summer garden party.

Marinated and Grilled Salmon
4 (4-ounce) salmon fillets
1/2 teaspoon granulated garlic
2 teaspoons salt
1/2 teaspoon pepper
1/4 cup olive oil

Salad
16 ounces mixed salad greens
1/2 cup (2 ounces) grated Parmesan cheese
1/4 cup chopped fresh dill weed
1/2 cup balsamic vinaigrette
salt and pepper to taste
1/2 red onion, thinly sliced
12 cherry tomatoes, cut into halves
1/2 European cucumber, sliced

Garnish
4 lemon wedges
1 tablespoon chopped fresh dill weed

For the salmon, place the fillets in a shallow dish. Mix the granulated garlic, salt and pepper in a bowl. Season both sides of the salmon fillets with the mixture and brush evenly with the olive oil. Let stand for 30 minutes.

Preheat a gas grill or charcoal grill. Spray both sides of the salmon with nonstick cooking spray. Grill for 3 minutes on each side or just until cooked through.

For the salad, combine the mixed greens, Parmesan cheese and dill weed in a large bowl. Add the balsamic vinaigrette and toss lightly to coat evenly. Season with salt and pepper. Spoon evenly onto four serving plates.

Arrange the onion, cherry tomatoes and cucumber over and around the salads and place 1 salmon fillet on each salad. Garnish the salmon with a lemon wedge and additional chopped dill weed.

You can sauté the salmon for this dish rather than grilling it if you prefer.

Serves four

Wine Master's Suggestion: Biltmore Pinot Noir

Beef Tenderloin Display

Tenderloin
1 (2 1/2-pound) beef tenderloin, trimmed
1 cup Meat Rub (below)
2 tablespoons extra-virgin olive oil

Roasted Tomatoes
6 Roma tomatoes
2 tablespoons extra-virgin olive oil
2 tablespoons chopped fresh basil, or
    1 teaspoon dried basil
salt and pepper to taste

Arugula
1 tablespoon extra-virgin olive oil
1 teaspoon fresh lemon juice
1 teaspoon kosher salt
1/4 teaspoon cracked pepper
3 cups baby arugula

Assembly
1 1/2 cups (6 ounces) crumbled blue cheese
1/2 red onion, shaved
1/2 cup kalamata olives

For the tenderloin, preheat the oven to 375 degrees. Sear the tenderloin until golden brown on all sides in a small amount of olive oil in a heated skillet. Rub with a paste of the Meat Rub and 2 tablespoons olive oil. Place on a rack in a roasting pan and insert a meat thermometer into the thickest portion. Roast for 25 to 40 minutes or to 125 degrees on the meat thermometer. Cool completely.

For the tomatoes, reduce the oven temperature to 350 degrees. Core and cut the tomatoes into halves and combine with the olive oil, basil, salt and pepper in a bowl; toss to coat well. Place on a rack in a roasting pan. Roast for 15 to 20 minutes. Cool completely.

For the arugula, mix the olive oil, lemon juice, kosher salt and pepper in a bowl. Add the arugula and toss to coat evenly.

To assemble, spoon the arugula on a large platter. Slice the beef and arrange it in a row down the center of the platter. Arrange the roasted tomatoes, blue cheese, onion and olives in rows on the platter. Serve with focaccia bread or other bread.

Serves six to eight   *Wine Master's Suggestion*: Biltmore Château Reserve Cabernet Franc

Meat Rub

1 teaspoon granulated garlic
1 teaspoon granulated onion
1 teaspoon dried chives
1/2 teaspoon fennel seeds
1/4 teaspoon celery seeds

1/4 teaspoon dried thyme
1/4 teaspoon dried tarragon
1/4 cup kosher salt
1 tablespoon cracked black pepper
1/4 teaspoon crushed red pepper

Combine the granulated garlic, granulated onion, chives, fennel seeds, celery seeds, thyme, tarragon, kosher salt, black pepper and red pepper in a small bowl. Use as a dry rub for meat. You can also mix the rub with 2 tablespoons olive oil to make a paste if you prefer.

Makes about 1 cup

Grilled Marinated Flank Steak with Mango and Black Bean Salsa

Season the grill for this recipe by applying a thin coat of oil to the grill rack to avoid sticking. Moving the steak soon after it is placed on the grill will result in sticking even if the grill has been seasoned, so be sure to leave it alone until it is ready to be turned. You can substitute other cuts of beef for the flank steak in this recipe, such as rib-eye, strip or tenderloin.

1 (1¹/₂- to 2-pound) flank steak
4 cups Flank Steak Marinade (below)
2 tablespoons vegetable oil

¹/₃ cup Meat Rub (page page 71)
Mango and Black Bean Salsa (page 58)

Combine the flank steak with the Flank Steak Marinade in a 1-gallon sealable plastic bag, coating the steak well. Marinate in the refrigerator for 12 hours.

Preheat the grill to very hot, but with a low flame, and coat the grill rack with the vegetable oil. Drain the steak and blot with paper towels to absorb the moisture. Coat evenly with the Meat Rub, rubbing it in. Place the steak on the hottest part of the grill and grill for 3 to 4 minutes. Turn the steak and move to a less hot part of the grill. Grill to an internal temperature of 120 on an instant-read thermometer. Remove to a chopping board and let stand for 12 minutes.

Cut the steak into thin slices. Spoon the Mango and Black Bean Salsa onto a serving plate and arrange the steak slices in a fan pattern on the salsa.

Serves four to six

Wine Master's Suggestion: Biltmore Syrah

Flank Steak Marinade

2 cups beef broth
¹/₄ cup balsamic vinegar
1 tablespoon soy sauce
4 dashes Tabasco sauce
2 tablespoons chopped garlic
　(about 2 garlic cloves)

1 shallot, minced
1 tablespoon dried rosemary
1 teaspoon dried oregano
1¹/₂ teaspoons kosher salt
2 teaspoons coarsely ground pepper

Combine the beef broth, vinegar, soy sauce and Tabasco sauce in a bowl. Add the garlic, shallot, rosemary, oregano, kosher salt and pepper and mix well.

Makes 2¹/₂ cups

Carolina Pulled Pork

Carolina pulled pork is a venerable tradition in western North Carolina. Once the sole purview of artisan pit masters, this recipe brings the authentic taste of Carolina barbecue to your own backyard. Real barbecue in the absence of a barbecue pit requires first smoking and then slow-roasting.

2 cups apple cider
2 cups apple cider vinegar
2 ancho chiles
Pork Rub (page 74)
1 (7- to 8-pound) Boston butt pork shoulder

Combine the apple cider, cider vinegar and ancho chiles in a saucepan. Simmer for 20 minutes; strain and let stand to cool.

Reserve 1/2 cup of the Pork Rub for the final seasoning. Rub the pork liberally with the remaining Pork Rub. Wrap in plastic wrap and place in the refrigerator until ready to smoke.

To smoke the pork, preheat a barrel smoker by filling the water container with hot water and preparing a small charcoal fire below it. You can use a Weber-style grill if it is large enough to smoke the pork over indirect heat. Place the pork in the top of the smoker and add chunks (not chips) of hardwood, such as oak, hickory or apple, on the smoker to produce a good smoke. Smoke the pork for 6 hours or to a dark caramel color, maintaining a temperature not to exceed 225 degrees.

To slow-roast the pork, preheat the oven to 250 degrees. Place the pork on a rack in a small roasting pan and tent with foil. Roast for 2 to 3 hours or until you can stick a fork into the pork and turn the fork 180 degrees with minimal effort.

Remove to a carving board and let stand for 1 hour. Pull or chop the pork into small pieces, discarding the bone. Season with 3/4 cup of the cider mixture and the reserved Meat Rub. Serve as is or with barbecue sauce. Reserve unused cider mixture for another purpose.

Serves twelve

Wine Master's Suggestion: Biltmore Cardinal's Crest

Picnics

Picnics were a popular summer pastime on the 125,000-acre Biltmore Estate. Nineteenth-century sources recommended that picnic provisions always include horseradish, mint sauce, salad dressing, vinegar, mustard, pepper, salt, good oil, sugar, ice, wine glasses, teacups and saucers, as well as several teapots and corkscrews. Biltmore's food service collections include a wicker picnic trunk that opened to reveal an interior fitted for various food tins, utensils, cups, and plates. Other pieces include a black canvas-covered picnic trunk, a two-handled wicker wine casket, and three stainless-steel picnic boxes for transporting food.

Barbecued Spareribs

Debates over what constitutes a great barbecued rib can take on religious proportions. The Stable Café's interpretation of the perfect sparerib is sweet, spicy, smoky, and almost fallin'-off-the-bone tender. This must be what people think about when they say, "There is no such thing as a bad rib."

3 slabs St. Louis-style spareribs
Pork Rub (below)
barbecue sauce

Prepare an indirect smoker or barrel smoker by building a small charcoal fire in the fire box and adding 2 or 3 chunks (not shavings) of oak or hickory. Heat to 250 degrees. You can also use a Weber-type grill if you build a very small fire at one end of the grill and cook the ribs at the other end.

Rub each rib generously with the Pork Rub. Place the ribs on the grill and smoke for 2 1/4 hours, maintaining a constant 250-degree temperature. Brush with your favorite barbecue sauce and smoke for 10 minutes longer or until tender.

Serves four   *Wine Master's Suggestion*: Biltmore Red Zinfandel

Pork Rub

1 cup packed brown sugar
1/4 cup granulated garlic
1/4 cup granulated onion
1/4 cup Montreal Steak Seasoning
2 tablespoons dry mustard
2 tablespoons ground cumin
1/3 cup salt
1/4 cup pepper

For the rub, combine the brown sugar, granulated garlic, granulated onion, Montreal Steak Seasoning, dry mustard, cumin, salt and pepper in a bowl; mix well.

Montreal Steak Seasoning is available in most food markets.

Makes about 2 1/2 cups

Papaver flore pleno

Grilled Chicken Pita Sandwich

3 pounds boneless skinless chicken breasts, cut into 1-inch cubes
1 red onion, cut into 1-inch pieces
1 green bell pepper, cut into 1-inch pieces
1 red bell pepper, cut into 1-inch pieces
1 cup pineapple juice
1/2 cup soy sauce
1/2 cup Biltmore Chardonnay Sur Lies
1/2 cup olive oil
6 pita rounds
Sun-Dried Tomato Spread (below)

Thread the chicken, onion and bell peppers onto skewers. Mix the pineapple juice, soy sauce and wine in a shallow dish. Add the skewers and marinate in the refrigerator for 1 hour or longer, turning occasionally.

Preheat a grill. Brush the chicken lightly with some of the olive oil and grill the skewers until the chicken is cooked through; brush with the remaining olive oil. Grill the pita rounds for 1 minute on each side.

Cut the pita rounds into halves and spread to form pockets. Spread the Sun-Dried Tomato Spread in the pockets and add the grilled chicken and vegetables. Serve immediately.

Serves twelve   *Wine Master's Suggestion*: Biltmore Cardinal's Crest

Sun-Dried Tomato Spread

1/2 cup sun-dried tomatoes
1/2 cup pitted kalamata olives
2 tablespoons goat cheese
1/2 cup olive oil
1/4 cup balsamic vinegar
1 small bunch fresh basil

Combine the sun-dried tomatoes, olives, goat cheese, olive oil, balsamic vinegar and basil in a food processor. Process to form a smooth paste. Store in the refrigerator until needed.

Makes about two cups

Sautéed Grouper with Vegetables Provençal and Bacon Butter

Vegetables Provençal
2 cups drained canned artichoke hearts
1 cup (1/2-inch strips) roasted
    red bell pepper
1 cup (1/2-inch strips) roasted
    yellow bell pepper
6 shallots, cut into halves and roasted
10 garlic cloves, roasted
1 cup kalamata olive halves
2 cups grape tomato halves
1 tablespoon coarsely chopped fresh basil
1 tablespoon coarsely chopped
    fresh oregano
1 tablespoon salt

1 1/2 teaspoons pepper
1/4 cup Champagne vinegar
1/4 cup extra-virgin olive oil

Grouper
8 (5-ounce) grouper fillets, or other
    white fish fillets
salt and white pepper to taste
olive oil
Bacon Butter (below)

Garnish
chopped fresh herbs

For the vegetables, combine the artichoke hearts, bell peppers, shallots, garlic, olives and tomatoes in a large bowl. Add the basil and oregano and season with the salt and pepper. Stir in the vinegar and olive oil. Refrigerate until time to serve.

For the grouper, preheat the oven to 350 degrees. Sprinkle the fillets with salt and white pepper. Sear in olive oil in a large ovenproof skillet for 2 minutes on each side. Place in the oven and bake for 15 minutes or until cooked through.

Spoon the vegetables into a heated sauté pan and cook until heated through. Spoon into the centers of eight serving plates and place 1 fillet on each. Top with Bacon Butter and garnish with chopped herbs. Serve immediately.

Serves eight   *Wine Master's Suggestion*: Biltmore Methode Champenoise Blanc de Noir Brut

Bacon Butter

4 slices bacon, chopped
1 shallot, minced
1 garlic clove, minced
6 tablespoons rice wine vinegar

6 tablespoons heavy cream
1/2 cup (1 stick) unsalted butter, chopped
salt and white pepper to taste

Sauté the bacon in a sauté pan until crisp; drain. Combine the shallot, garlic and vinegar in a saucepan and cook until most of the liquid has evaporated. Add the cream and bacon and cook until reduced by 3/4. Whisk in the butter and season with salt and white pepper. Spoon into a small bowl. Store, covered, in the refrigerator until time to serve.

Serves eight

Grilled Summer Vegetable and Goat Cheese Pizzetas

Pizza Dough (below)
2 heirloom tomatoes
1 red onion
1 small zucchini
1 small yellow squash
2 portobello mushrooms

1/2 cup olive oil
1 tablespoon chopped garlic
salt and freshly ground pepper to taste
1/2 cup crumbled goat cheese
12 basil leaves, thinly sliced

Preheat a grill to hot, allowing 10 to 15 minutes to heat. Place each portion of the Pizza Dough on an inverted cake pan or baking pan and press gently into a circle. Invert the pans on the grill so that the dough circles rest on the grill. Grill for 1 to 2 minutes or until the dough is set. Remove the pans and turn the crusts over. Grill until the other side is marked. Remove from the grill.

Cut the tomatoes, onion, zucchini, yellow squash and mushrooms into chunks. Combine with the olive oil, garlic, salt and pepper in a bowl and toss to coat evenly. Grill the vegetables until tender-crisp. Chop into bite-size pieces and sprinkle over the pizza crusts. Sprinkle the goat cheese over the vegetables.

Preheat the oven to 400 degrees. Bake the pizzetas until the cheese melts and the crusts are crisp. Sprinkle with the basil. Cut into wedges to serve.

Makes four or five pizzetas

Wine Master's Suggestion: Biltmore Sauvignon Blanc

Pizza Dough

2 3/4 cups all-purpose flour
1 tablespoon sugar
2 or 3 garlic cloves, minced
1 teaspoon dried basil
1 teaspoon dried rosemary
1 teaspoon dried tarragon
2 tablespoons olive oil
1/4 cup vegetable oil
1/2 teaspoon salt
1 tablespoon quick-rising dry yeast
1 cup warm water

Combine the flour, sugar, garlic, basil, rosemary, tarragon, olive oil, vegetable oil and salt in a mixing bowl; mix with a dough hook. Add the yeast and mix at low speed. Add 1/2 cup of the water gradually, mixing constantly. Add the remaining water gradually, mixing constantly until the dough pulls away from the side of the bowl. Mix at low to medium speed for 3 to 4 minutes longer.

Remove to an oiled bowl, turning to coat the surface. Let rise, covered with a clean towel, until doubled in bulk. Punch down the dough and let rise again until doubled in bulk. Punch down to remove air bubbles and divide into 4 to 5 equal portions.

Makes four or five pizzeta crusts

Hours before butlers delivered breakfast trays to the Vanderbilts and their guests in their rooms, farm and dairy households had dished up fried eggs with potatoes, bacon, sausage, and biscuits fresh from the wood-burning oven dripping with butter and jam. Likewise, they prepared hearty midday dinners complete with meat, gravy, potatoes, fresh or home-canned vegetables, corn bread or biscuits, and a piping hot fruit cobbler well before luncheon appeared on the Breakfast Room table. Farm suppers were the lightest meal of the day, unlike the multi-course dinners in "the big house," as estate families affectionately came to call Biltmore House.

Tomato Vidalia Gratin

Vidalia onions are a naturally sweet variety of onion grown in Vidalia, Georgia. If Vidalia onions are not available, yellow or white onions can be used in this recipe, but they will not have as much sweetness.

1 unbaked (9- inch) deep-dish pie shell
1 very large slicing tomato, sliced
1/2 cup chopped fresh basil
1 cup chopped Vidalia onion
1 cup (4 ounces) shredded Cheddar cheese
1 cup (4 ounces) shredded mozzarella cheese
1/2 cup mayonnaise, or enough to bind the mixture
1 pound bacon, crisp-fried and chopped
1/2 teaspoon pepper

Preheat the oven to 350 degrees. Bake the pie shell for 8 minutes or just until light brown. Cool for 5 minutes. Arrange the tomato slices in the pie shell and sprinkle with the basil and onion.

Mix the Cheddar cheese, mozzarella cheese, mayonnaise and bacon in a bowl. Season with the pepper. Press the cheese mixture over the vegetables. Bake for 20 to 25 minutes or until golden brown. Cool for 5 to 10 minutes before serving.

Serves four to six

Paeonia lactiflora

Corn Muffins

Our corn muffins are a little different than you may have had in the past. The addition of the cream-style corn is a very important element and makes for a moist cake-like corn muffin.

1 cup milk
1 cup vegetable oil
2 eggs
2 cups cream-style corn
1/4 cup sugar
1 tablespoon kosher salt
1 teaspoon pepper
1 1/2 cups all-purpose flour, sifted
2 teaspoons baking powder
1 1/4 cups cornmeal

Preheat the oven to 350 degrees. Whisk together the milk, oil, eggs, corn, sugar, kosher salt and pepper in a bowl. Add the flour, baking powder and cornmeal and whisk just until combined. Spoon into muffin cups sprayed with nonstick cooking spray, filling 2/3 full. Bake for 25 to 35 minutes or until golden brown. Serve warm.

Makes two dozen

ATELETTES.
1. Crayfish, ornamentally cut, Mushrooms, and Truffles.—2. Button Mushrooms, Cockscombs, and Truffles.—3. Mushroom, Prawns, and Truffles.—4. Star of Aspic Jelly with centre of Barberries, surrounded by rings of Carrot, with Green Peas in the rings; Green Peas and ornamented Mushrooms.—5. Ornamented Mushrooms, Truffles, Green Peas, Parsley and Carrots, and Parsnips cut in miniature.—6. Ornamented Mushroom, Truffles, Green Peas, Parsley and Carrots, and Parsnips cut in miniature.—7. Aspic Jelly shape, ornamental centre of Green Peas and Carrots, Truffles and Crayfish.—8. Aspic Jelly shape, centred with Barberries and rings of Green Peas, Truffles, and rounds of Carrots.

The Biltmore House Library contains a cookbook, The Encyclopaedia of Practical Cookery, published at the turn of the last century. Recipes for Asparagus Soup, Glazed Carrots, or Peach Cobbler could have incorporated estate-grown produce. Some, such as Roast Loin of Pork and Baked Saddle of Lamb, would have featured estate-raised livestock. Others, such as Broiled Pigeon, Stewed Venison, and Rabbit a'l'Italienne, called for wild game. Some recipes, like the Terrine of Duck Livers, were very elaborate, while others were for such simple dishes as Griddle Cakes and Soda Biscuits, prepared in mountain kitchens all over western North Carolina.

The Market Garden

The Market Garden was located in fertile bottomland near the confluence of the French Broad and Swannanoa Rivers. The complex included greenhouses and forcing houses, as well as a cottage for the Market Gardener's family. Adjacent to the cottage was a courtyard where produce was prepared for delivery to Biltmore House and the Biltmore Store in nearby Biltmore Village, or to be sold wholesale to local markets. Gardeners experimented with numerous varieties of vegetables to find the ones that produced the best results. Some more unusual vegetables included artichokes, kohlrabi, chicory, salsify, Egyptian beets, and Siberian kale.

Blackberries

For farm and dairy families, summer's pleasures included picking blackberries. Ruby Redmon recalled,

"Momma never canned less than a hundred quarts . . . the blackberries on Biltmore Estate was a staple for a lot of families, because you not only had your jellies, you also had your pies and cobblers . . . And then her sisters' children would come and pick, so it seemed like the more that came to pick the more you had. The Lord always supplied a lot. And that's what I think I miss the most. You don't get anything that tasted like they did."

Blueberry Scones with Lemon Curd

Lemon Curd
5 egg yolks
1 cup lemon juice
1 cup sugar
1/3 stick butter

Scones
1 1/2 cups all-purpose flour
1 1/2 teaspoons sugar
1/2 teaspoon baking powder
1/2 teaspoon salt
1/2 cup (1 stick) butter, sliced
3/4 cup dried blueberries
grated zest of 1/2 lemon
3/4 cup heavy cream

For the curd, combine the egg yolks, lemon juice, sugar and butter in a double boiler. Cook over simmering water until thickened, whisking constantly. Strain through a fine sieve into a bowl. Place the bowl in an ice bath to chill.

For the scones, preheat the oven to 350 degrees. Combine the flour, sugar, baking powder and salt in a mixing bowl and mix at low speed with a paddle attachment. Add the butter and mix well. Add the dried blueberries and lemon zest, then the cream, pulsing just until the dough comes together; do not overmix.

Roll on a lightly floured surface and cut into triangles. Place on a baking sheet and brush with additional cream. Bake until the edges are golden brown. Serve with Lemon Curd.

Makes fifteen to twenty

Blackberry Cobbler

Add your own touch to this cobbler by sprinkling the top with nuts, cinnamon-sugar, or other toppings before baking.

1 (21-ounce) can blackberry pie filling
16 ounces fresh or frozen blackberries
2 2/3 cups all-purpose flour
1 cup sugar
1 tablespoon baking powder
1 1/2 teaspoons salt

1/4 cup vegetable oil
1 egg
1 cup milk
splash of vanilla extract
 (about 1/6 teaspoon)

Preheat the oven to 350 degrees. Spread the pie filling in a greased 9×13-inch baking pan. Sprinkle the whole blackberries over the filling.

Combine the flour, sugar, baking powder and salt in a bowl. Add the oil, egg, milk and vanilla and whisk just until combined; the batter may be lumpy. Spread over the berries. Bake for 50 minutes.

Serves eight   *Wine Master's Suggestion*: Biltmore Winemaker's Selection Chenin Blanc

Strawberry Pie

Crumb Topping
1¼ cups all-purpose flour
½ cup packed brown sugar
¾ teaspoon cinnamon
½ cup (1 stick) butter, sliced

Pie
1 unbaked (10-inch) pie shell
1¼ cups sugar
½ cup plus 2 tablespoons bread flour
¾ teaspoon cinnamon
¼ teaspoon salt
2 quarts strawberries, cut into quarters
1 tablespoon lemon juice
2 tablespoons butter, melted
2 tablespoons milk
1 teaspoon vanilla extract

Garnish
whipped cream
mint sprigs

For the topping, combine the flour, brown sugar, cinnamon and butter in a bowl. Mix with your fingers until crumbly.

For the pie, preheat the oven to 350 degrees. Bake the pie shell for 8 minutes or just until it begins to brown. Mix the sugar, bread flour, cinnamon and salt in a bowl. Add the strawberries and toss to coat evenly. Add the lemon juice, melted butter, milk and vanilla and mix gently. Spoon into the pie shell and sprinkle with the topping. Bake for 1 hour. Garnish each serving with a dollop of whipped cream and a mint sprig.

Serves six to eight

Wine Master's Suggestion:
Biltmore Methode Champenoise Blanc de Noir Brut

Rosa alba plena flore

Peanut Butter Pie

This is a very popular dessert at the Stable Café Restaurant. Use only high-quality chocolate, such a Ghiradelli, Valrhona, or Cocoa Barry for this recipe and do not substitute chocolate chips for couverture.

Pie
14 ounces cream cheese, softened
2 cups sugar
1 1/2 cups creamy peanut butter
1 tablespoon vanilla extract
2 tablespoons unsalted butter, melted
1 cup heavy whipping cream
1 chocolate cookie pie shell

Chocolate Ganache
1 cup heavy whipping cream
8 ounces semisweet chocolate couverture,
  finely chopped

For the pie, beat the cream cheese and sugar in a mixing bowl with a paddle attachment until smooth, scraping down the side as needed. Add the peanut butter and vanilla and mix well. Beat in the melted butter gradually.

Whip the cream in a mixing bowl with a whip attachment until soft peaks form. Fold into the peanut butter mixture. Spread in the pie shell and chill in the refrigerator.

For the ganache, bring the cream to a boil in a saucepan. Pour over the chocolate in a bowl. Stir gently to melt the chocolate and mix well. Cool slightly and spread evenly over the pie. Chill until serving time. Cut with a knife that has been heated under hot water and wiped dry between slices.

Serves six to eight

Banana Slush Punch

6 small ripe bananas
1 (6-ounce) can frozen lemonade
1 (12-ounce) can frozen orange juice
1 (46-ounce) can pineapple juice
6 cups water
4 cups sugar
2 (2-liter) bottles of ginger ale

Purée the bananas in a blender. Add the frozen lemonade and frozen orange juice; process until smooth. Combine with the pineapple juice, water and sugar in a container and mix well. Add the ginger ale just before serving.

Serves twenty-five

Fleur d'ange.

*W*hen summer ends,

the North Carolina skies

become a brilliant, transparent blue

with the first hint of crisp weather

and the signs of a

plentiful harvest to come.

The mountains glow with

the colors of autumn—

fiery oranges and yellows,

russets, and burgundies.

Autumn

organized, a season for the one

generation to teach the next about

the smoking of meats, the cooking

of game, the drying of shuck beans

and apples, and the pressing of

cider. In Biltmore's farm cottages,

gatherings around the table were

welcoming and warm after a hard

*W*hen summer ends, the North Carolina skies

become a brilliant, transparent blue with the first hint of

crisp weather and the signs of a plentiful harvest to

come. The mountains glow with the colors of autumn—

fiery oranges and yellows, russets, and burgundies.

It is a time of hard work and celebration, a season for

preparing and putting aside the cords of wood, the jars

of vegetables and jams and jellies accounted for and

day's labor, and plates were passed in thanksgiving and gratitude for friends and family. In Biltmore

House, fires were lit and tea was poured; books from the Library were shared aloud; and George

Vanderbilt's friends retreated to the Billiard Room for after-dinner cigars and fine brandy. Couples drifted

outside to the Loggia to feel the brisk autumn air and to enjoy the round full moon lighting the hills and

valleys below. Some ventured out for an evening carriage ride, bundled underneath warm woolen blankets.

Lingering as long as they could to enjoy the conversation, guests would finally bid one another good

night. Upstairs, thick down comforters were layered on beds, and bedroom fireplaces crackled with the

sounds and smells of an October evening.

Autumn Harvest Menu

Fennel and Tomato Soup

Roasted Quail with Country Bacon Jus

Lemon Grits

Apple Tart

Roasted Quail with Lemon Grits and Country Bacon Jus

Wild Mushroom Bruschetta

1 pound shiitake mushrooms
1 pound cremini mushrooms
1 pound oyster mushrooms
1 pound button mushrooms
1/2 cup olive oil
1/2 cup minced garlic
4 shallots, chopped
1/2 cup (1 stick) butter, melted
1 cup marsala wine
2 cups canned whole tomatoes

2 tablespoons chopped fresh basil
1 tablespoon chopped fresh oregano
3 tablespoons chopped fresh parsley
1 tablespoon salt
1 1/2 teaspoons pepper
2 loaves French bread
melted butter
1 cup (4 ounces) grated Parmesan cheese
4 cups (16 ounces) shredded Gouda cheese

Preheat the oven to 400 degrees. Sauté the mushrooms in the olive oil in a heated saucepan. Sweat the garlic and shallots in 1/2 cup butter in a saucepan until tender. Add the mushrooms and sauté for 5 minutes. Add the wine, stirring to deglaze the saucepan. Cook until the liquid evaporates. Drain the tomatoes and press to remove any excess liquid. Add to the mushroom mixture and then stir in the basil, oregano and parsley. Season with the salt and pepper.

Cut the bread into halves lengthwise and brush the cut sides with melted butter. Place on a baking sheet and bake for 3 minutes. Spread the mushroom mixture on the bread and top with the Parmesan cheese and Gouda cheese. Broil just until the cheeses melt. Slice to serve.

Serves four to six

George Washington Vanderbilt first visited Asheville, North Carolina, in 1888. He was a world traveler, ardent bibliophile, and avid collector of prints and other fine and decorative art. This is one of his last formal portraits, taken in 1914, just prior to his untimely death on March 6 at the age of 51.

George married Edith Stuyvesant Dresser on June 1, 1898, in Paris. Here, Edith is seen in one of a series of engagement photographs taken in Paris.

Sweet Potato Mulligatawny

1/2 cup (1 stick) butter
4 cups chopped yellow onions
2 cups chopped red bell peppers
1/4 cup finely chopped jalapeño chiles
kosher salt to taste
1/4 cup minced garlic
1/4 cup minced ginger
2 tablespoons cumin seeds, toasted and ground
3 tablespoons coriander seeds, toasted and ground
1/4 cup curry powder
1/2 teaspoon crushed red pepper
1 cup sherry
1/4 cup all-purpose flour
10 cups chicken broth
2 1/4 pounds sweet potatoes, peeled and chopped
1 (14-ounce) can coconut milk
2 cups orange juice
1/2 cup lime juice
3/4 cup heavy cream
2 pounds pulled cooked chicken
1/3 cup chopped cilantro

Garnish
crumbled goat cheese

Melt the butter in a large stockpot over medium heat. Add the onions, bell peppers, jalapeño chiles and kosher salt and sauté for 1 minute. Add the garlic and ginger and sauté for 8 to 10 minutes or until the vegetables are tender and light brown. Stir in the cumin, coriander, curry powder and crushed red pepper. Sauté for 2 minutes. Add the sherry, stirring to deglaze the stockpot. Cook until the mixture is reduced by 90 percent and is almost dry.

Add the flour and whisk to incorporate well. Cook for 1 minute. Whisk in the chicken broth and then stir in the sweet potatoes. Bring to a boil, stirring constantly. Reduce the heat and simmer until the sweet potatoes are tender.

Process the mixture with an immersion blender or in a food processor until smooth. Stir in the coconut milk, orange juice, lime juice and cream. Return to the stockpot if using a food processor. Add the chicken and cilantro and season with kosher salt. Cook until heated through. Ladle into soup bowls and garnish with goat cheese. Serve with grilled pita rounds.

Serves twelve

Wine Master's Suggestion: Biltmore Dry Riesling

Fennel and Tomato Soup

1 fennel bulb, chopped
1/2 yellow onion, chopped
1 bunch leeks, chopped
1 garlic clove, minced
1/4 cup (1/2 stick) butter, melted
1/4 teaspoon crushed red pepper
1/2 teaspoon anise seeds
1/4 cup marsala wine
1/4 cup all-purpose flour
1/2 gallon (8 cups) chicken stock
2 (15-ounce) cans diced tomatoes
3/4 cup heavy cream
1 tablespoon sugar
1 1/2 teaspoons kosher salt
1 teaspoon ground black pepper
1 tablespoon chopped fresh basil
1 tablespoon chopped fresh oregano

Garnish
chopped fresh herbs
croutons
grated Parmesan cheese

Sweat the fennel, onion, leeks and garlic in the butter in a saucepan until tender and translucent. Add the crushed red pepper and anise seeds and sauté for 1 minute. Add the wine, stirring to deglaze the saucepan. Cook until reduced by 3/4.

Add the flour and stir until smooth. Cook for 1 minute, stirring constantly. Whisk in the chicken stock and then add the tomatoes. Simmer for 15 minutes, stirring frequently. Remove from the heat and purée the mixture in a food processor or with an immersion blender. Return to the heat and stir in the cream, sugar, kosher salt and black pepper. Finish with the basil and oregano. Ladle into heated soup bowls and garnish with chopped fresh herbs, croutons and grated Parmesan cheese.

Serves six

Fall Salad

1 tablespoon lemon juice
1 tablespoon sugar
2 cups water
1 1/2 Granny Smith apples
16 ounces mixed salad greens
1 cup plus 2 tablespoons
    Biltmore Vinaigrette (below)
1 1/2 cups crumbled blue cheese
12 slices bacon, crisp-fried and crumbled
1 1/2 cups caramelized walnuts
15 cherry tomatoes, cut into halves

Combine the lemon juice, sugar and water in a 2-quart bowl and whisk until the sugar dissolves. Cut the apples into thin wedges and place in the lemon water to prevent browning.

Toss the mixed greens with Biltmore Vinaigrette and the blue cheese in a large stainless steel bowl. Spoon onto 6 plates. Sprinkle with the bacon and caramelized walnuts. Add 5 cherry tomato halves to each serving and top evenly with the apples. Serve immediately.

Serves six   *Wine Master's Suggestion*: Biltmore Signature Napa Valley Chardonnay

Biltmore Vinaigrette

1 egg
1 cup mustard
2 tablespoons Worcestershire sauce
2 tablespoons sugar
1 tablespoon minced garlic in oil
2 teaspoons paprika
1 tablespoon salt
1 1/2 teaspoons white pepper
4 cups vegetable oil
1 cup cider vinegar

Combine the egg, mustard, Worcestershire sauce, sugar, garlic, paprika, salt and white pepper in a food processor and process until smooth. Add the oil and vinegar at the same time in 2 gradual streams, processing to mix well.

The Biltmore makes this dressing with Gulden's Mustard. If you prefer not to use uncooked egg, substitute an equal amount of pasteurized egg.

Makes five and one-half cups

"Modern" Conveniences

Biltmore's kitchen staff employed many conveniences. A hand-cranked "state-of-the-art" Starrett Hasher, made for chopping meat, was the forerunner of the modern food processor. A Universal bread maker, also cranked by hand, kneaded bread dough. A giant marble mortar and pestle ground cinnamon and other spices for luncheon's apple tarts. Café noir, or black coffee, served at the end of every dinner, was brewed from beans freshly ground in an Enterprise coffee mill. Fresh from the estate butcher, pork from purebred Berkshire hogs raised at the Pig Farm could be made into breakfast links using the Enterprise sausage stuffer.

Pot Roast

Pot roast served with mashed potatoes and gravy is a perfect fall or winter dish. It defines what we think of as comfort food.

2 cups Biltmore Red Zinfandel
1/4 cup balsamic vinegar
1/4 cup honey
4 large carrots, peeled and coarsely chopped
4 celery ribs, coarsely chopped
5 white onions, coarsely chopped
1 bundle thyme, tied with kitchen twine
salt and freshly ground pepper to taste
1 (5-pound) boneless chuck roast
2 cups no-salt-added beef broth, or as needed

Combine the wine, balsamic vinegar and honey in a large bowl. Add the carrots, celery, onions, thyme, salt and pepper and mix well. Add the roast, coating well with the wine mixture. Marinate, covered, in the refrigerator for 12 to 24 hours.

Preheat the oven to 350 degrees. Drain the roast and vegetables, reserving the marinade. Place the roast and vegetables in an ovenproof pan and season with salt and pepper. Roast for 30 to 45 minutes or until dark brown.

Strain the reserved marinade and pour it over the roast and vegetables. Add enough beef broth to cover the roast. Bring to a simmer on the stovetop and simmer for 5 minutes, skimming the surface of any impurities; do not boil.

Braise in the oven for 2 to 3 hours or until very tender. Remove the roast to a platter and discard the thyme bundle. Process the cooking liquid and vegetables in a food processor until smooth and strain through a fine mesh sieve. Return to the pan and simmer until reduced to gravy consistency. Add the roast to the gravy and break into serving portions with a fork. Cook until heated through.

Serves six to eight

Wine Master's Suggestion: Biltmore Red Century

Veal Osso Buco with Sherried Veal Jus

Gremolata is the traditional garnish for osso buco.

Osso Buco
6 veal foreshanks
1/4 cup salt
2 teaspoons pepper
1/2 cup all-purpose flour
1/2 cup vegetable oil
2 yellow onions, chopped
4 ribs celery, chopped
5 carrots, peeled and chopped
2 cups sherry
1 gallon (16 cups) veal stock
1 cup canned whole tomatoes,
   drained and pressed to remove
   any excess liquid
3 bay leaves
1 bunch parsley
2 thyme sprigs
salt and pepper to taste

Gremolata
1 bunch parsley, chopped
1/4 cup chopped garlic
grated zest of 2 lemons
1 teaspoon salt
1/2 teaspoon pepper

For the osso buco, season the veal shanks with 1/4 cup salt and 2 teaspoons pepper and coat lightly with the flour. Heat the vegetable oil in a skillet. Add the veal shanks in batches and cook until brown on all sides, removing to a platter as they brown.

Add the onions, celery and carrots to the drippings in the skillet and sauté until partially caramelized. Add the wine, stirring to deglaze the skillet. Cook until the wine has nearly evaporated.

Combine the vegetable mixture with the veal stock, tomatoes, bay leaves, parsley and thyme in a large saucepan. Bring to a boil and add the veal shanks. Reduce the heat to medium-low and simmer for 3 hours or until the veal is fork-tender. Season with salt and pepper. Remove the veal shanks to serving plates. Strain the cooking liquid and serve with the veal.

For the gremolata, combine the parsley, garlic, lemon zest, salt and pepper in a bowl and mix well. Garnish the osso buco with the gremolata.

Serves six

Wine Master's Suggestion: Biltmore Sangiovese

Braised Short Ribs with Gingered Sweet Potato Mash and Cherry Barbecue Sauce

Short Ribs
4 (1½-pound) beef short ribs
salt and pepper to taste
2 tablespoons vegetable oil
8 ounces carrots, peeled and chopped
8 ounces celery, chopped
8 ounces white onions, chopped
2 quarts (8 cups) beef stock
2 ounces fresh thyme

Cherry Barbecue Sauce
reserved cooking liquid from
   the short ribs
1 tablespoon molasses
2 tablespoons tomato paste
2 tablespoons brown sugar
1 tablespoon Worcestershire sauce
2 tablespoons apple cider vinegar
½ cup dried sweet cherries
salt and pepper to taste

Assembly
Gingered Sweet Potato Mash (below)

For the short ribs, preheat the oven to 275 degrees. Season the short ribs with salt and pepper. Heat the oil in a large Dutch oven. Add the ribs and cook until brown on all sides; remove to a platter. Add the carrots, celery and onions to the drippings in the Dutch oven and cook until brown.

Return the ribs to the Dutch oven and add the beef stock and thyme. Braise, covered, in the oven for 3 hours or until the ribs are very tender. Remove the ribs to a platter; cover and keep warm. Strain and reserve the cooking liquid.

For the sauce, bring the reserved cooking liquid to a simmer in a medium saucepan. Cook until reduced by ½. Stir in the molasses, tomato paste, brown sugar, Worcestershire sauce, vinegar and dried cherries. Bring to a boil and reduce the heat to low. Simmer for 15 minutes. Season with salt and pepper.

To assemble, spoon the Gingered Sweet Potato Mash onto 4 serving plates. Place 1 short rib on each portion of sweet potatoes and drizzle with the Cherry Barbecue Sauce.

Serves four   *Wine Master's Suggestion*: Biltmore Signature North Coast Syrah

Gingered Sweet Potato Mash

2 pounds sweet potatoes, peeled
   and chopped
½ cup heavy cream
2 tablespoons butter

1 tablespoon grated ginger
¼ cup honey
salt and pepper to taste

Combine the sweet potatoes with enough cold water to cover in a large saucepan and cook until the sweet potatoes are tender. Combine the cream and butter in a saucepan and bring to a simmer; keep warm.

Drain the sweet potatoes. Combine with the ginger and push through a food mill or ricer. Mix with the warm cream mixture and honey in a bowl. Season with salt and pepper.

Serves four

Roasted Quail with Lemon Grits and Country Bacon Jus

Quail
4 semi-boneless quail
1 shallot, minced
2 garlic cloves, minced
salt and white pepper to taste
8 fresh sage leaves
2 tablespoons olive oil

Country Bacon Jus
1/4 cup chopped bacon
1/2 cup chopped onion
2 or 3 garlic cloves, minced

1/4 cup chopped peeled carrots
1/4 cup finely chopped celery
1 tablespoon tomato paste
1/4 cup Biltmore Château Reserve Claret
2 cups chicken broth
4 thyme sprigs
1 bay leaf
roasted quail legs and wings
2 tablespoons butter

Assembly
Lemon Grits (below)

For the quail, preheat the oven to 350 degrees. Remove the legs and wings from the quail, leaving the breasts intact. Place the legs and wings in a roasting pan and roast for 10 to 15 minutes. Reserve the legs and wings for the Country Bacon Jus.

Place the quail breasts skin side up on a work surface and separate the skin from the meat on one side of each to make pockets. Sprinkle the shallot, garlic, salt and white pepper lightly under the skin and add 2 sage leaves to each. Replace the skin, and roll the quail; tie into rolls with kitchen twine. Season the outside of the rolls with salt and white pepper.

Heat a skillet over medium-high heat and add the olive oil. Add the quail to the heated oil and sear on all sides. Place on a rack in a roasting pan and roast for 5 minutes.

For the country bacon jus, render the drippings from the bacon in a saucepan over medium heat for 5 minutes, stirring occasionally. Add the onion, garlic, carrots and celery. Sauté for 5 to 6 minutes. Add the tomato paste and cook until caramelized. Add the wine, stirring to deglaze the saucepan. Cook until the mixture is reduced by 1/2.

Add the chicken broth, thyme, bay leaf and roasted legs and wings. Cook until reduced by 3/4. Finish with the butter.

To assemble, spoon the Lemon Grits onto 4 serving plates. Slice the quail rolls and arrange on the grits. Remove the bay leaf from the Country Bacon Jus and drizzle the jus over the quail.

Serves four   *Wine Master's Suggestion*: Biltmore Château Reserve Claret

Lemon Grits

3 cups water
1 cup quick-cooking white grits
salt and freshly ground white pepper
   to taste

grated zest and juice of 2 or 3 lemons
butter to taste
8 ounces mascarpone cheese,
   or to taste

Bring the water to a boil in a saucepan. Whisk in the grits gradually. Cook over low heat for 15 to 20 minutes or until tender, stirring frequently. Season lightly with salt and white pepper. Stir in the lemon zest, lemon juice, butter and mascarpone cheese.

Serves four

Rotisserie Chicken

At the Stable Café, this is a time-honored method for cooking chicken. The sage brine allows for a deep penetration of flavor, making the chicken incredibly moist. We call the brine a quick brine because of its higher salt content, which allows the chicken to brine in one and one-half hours rather than twelve hours.

1 quart water
2 tablespoons granulated garlic
2 tablespoons granulated onion
2 tablespoons rubbed sage
1 cup packed brown sugar
2 cups kosher salt, or 1 2/3 cups iodized
   salt
3 quarts water
2 (3 1/2-pound) chickens
Chicken Rub (below)

Bring 1 quart water to a boil in a saucepan. Add the granulated garlic, granulated onion and sage. Remove from the heat and allow to stand for 20 minutes. Combine the brown sugar and salt with 3 quarts water in a large bowl and whisk to dissolve the brown sugar and salt. Add the steeped mixture and mix well.

Place the chickens in 2 sealable plastic bags in bowls and add the brine mixture. Seal the bags and place in the refrigerator for 1 1/2 hours.

Remove the chicken from the marinade, discarding the marinade. Season inside and out with the Chicken Rub. Place on a rotisserie and cook over medium-low heat for 2 1/2 hours or to an internal temperature of 160 degrees; the skin should be golden brown and crisp. You can also roast the chickens at 350 degrees for about 1 hour. Let the chickens stand for 30 minutes before serving.

Cut along both sides of the backbone with kitchen shears and remove the backbone. Turn the chicken over and slice along the breast bone to split the chickens into halves to serve.

Serves four   *Wine Master's Suggestion*: Biltmore Limited Release Merlot

Chicken Rub

1/4 cup granulated garlic
1/4 cup granulated onion
2 tablespoons paprika
2 teaspoons salt
1 tablespoon pepper

Mix the granulated garlic, granulated onion, paprika, salt and pepper in a bowl. Store in an airtight container. Use as a rub for chicken.

Makes about one-half cup

Shrimp and Grits

Tasso Gravy

6 ounces tasso, finely chopped
2 tablespoons butter, melted
1/2 cup chopped yellow onion
1/4 cup minced garlic
1/4 to 1/2 cup all-purpose flour
juice of 2 lemons
3/4 cup clam juice
1 cup heavy cream
4 tarragon sprigs, chopped
kosher salt and white pepper to taste

Shrimp

15 to 25 shrimp, peeled and deveined
kosher salt and white pepper to taste
olive oil
Grits (below)

Garnish

chopped parsley and tarragon

For the gravy, sauté the tasso in the butter in a heavy stockpot for 2 minutes. Add the onion and garlic and sauté for 3 minutes or until the onion is translucent. Add the flour and cook until bubbly, whisking constantly. Add the lemon juice, clam juice and cream. Reduce the heat and simmer until thickened, whisking constantly and adding additional cream if needed for the desired consistency. Season with the tarragon, kosher salt and white pepper.

For the shrimp, season the shrimp with kosher salt and white pepper. Sauté in a small amount of olive oil in a skillet. Add some of the tasso gravy and mix gently.

To serve, spoon Grits into serving bowls. Top with the shrimp and ladle additional tasso gravy over the top. Garnish with parsley and tarragon. Serve immediately.

Serves five

Wine Master's Suggestion: Biltmore Chardonnay sur Lies

Grits

You can substitute quick-cooking grits for the stone-ground grits and follow the instructions on the package if you prefer.

1 cup (2 sticks) butter
1/4 cup bacon drippings
16 cups water or chicken stock
4 cups uncooked stone-ground grits
1/2 cup milk

1/4 cup (1 ounce) grated Parmesan cheese
1/4 cup (1 ounce) shredded Monterey
   Jack cheese
chopped canned chipotle chiles to taste
2 tablespoons kosher salt

Combine the butter, bacon drippings and water in a large stockpot and bring to a boil. Add the grits and mix well, removing any impurities that float to the surface. Simmer over medium-low heat for 2 1/2 hours or until the grits are tender, stirring occasionally. Stir in the milk, Parmesan cheese, Monterey Jack cheese, chipotle chiles and kosher salt. Keep warm.

Serves twelve

The Art of Conversation

Guests were expected to converse throughout dinner, although comments about the food—even compliments—were considered déclassé. The host initiated conversation with the lady seated at his left, and this continued around the table, although by the end of the meal guests might be engaged in lively banter with diners on either side or across the table. Volatile topics such as religion or Darwinism were generally forbidden. Not everyone mastered the fine art of conversation, however, and many a boring or overbearing guest has been immortalized in the diaries of bemused or offended dining companions.

Crab and Artichoke-Crusted Salmon

This is a quick favorite and can be prepared ahead of time and finished just before serving.

1 shallot, minced
1 (14-ounce) can artichoke hearts, drained
2 garlic cloves, minced
1/2 cup (1 stick) unsalted butter, softened
4 ounces cream cheese, softened
1/4 cup (1 ounce) grated Parmesan cheese
4 ounces lump crab meat, drained and flaked
1/4 cup chopped fresh basil
1/4 cup thinly sliced chives
1/4 cup olive oil
6 (8-ounce) salmon fillets, skin removed
salt and pepper to taste

Preheat the oven to 375 degrees. Combine the shallot, artichoke hearts, garlic, butter, cream cheese and Parmesan cheese in a food processor. Process until mixed but not smooth. Add the crab meat, basil and chives and mix well.

Heat the olive oil in a large ovenproof sauté pan until it begins to shimmer. Season the salmon lightly with salt and pepper. Add to the sauté pan skin side up and sear until golden brown. Turn and sear the other side.

Spread about 1/2 cup of the crab mixture on each fillet. Bake for 5 to 8 minutes or until the salmon is firm and the crust is light brown. Serve immediately.

Serves six

Wine Master's Suggestion: Biltmore Pinot Noir

Brussels Sprouts with Vidalia Onions and Applewood Bacon

1 pound brussels sprouts
salt to taste
5 slices applewood-smoked bacon, julienned
1 tablespoon butter
1 Vidalia onion, chopped
2 teaspoons white vinegar
pepper to taste

Cook the brussels sprouts in salted water in a saucepan just until tender. Cook the bacon in a large sauté pan until the drippings are rendered and the bacon is crisp. Remove the bacon to a paper towel, reserving the drippings in the sauté pan. Add the butter and onion to the drippings and sauté until the onion is caramelized to a golden brown. Add the brussels sprouts, vinegar, salt and pepper. Cook until heated through. Sprinkle with the bacon to serve.

Serves two to four

Citrus Cranberry Relish

Fresh cranberries are usually available at food markets around Thanksgiving time. This relish is a wonderful accompaniment to turkey and pork.

12 ounces fresh cranberries
1 cup chopped fresh pineapple
1 1/2 cups mandarin oranges
3 tablespoons Triple Sec or Cointreau
1/2 cup sugar
1 cup pecans or walnuts, toasted, chopped and cooled

Combine the cranberries, pineapple, oranges, liqueur and sugar in a food processor and pulse until coarsely chopped. Chill in the refrigerator for 8 hours or longer to develop the flavor. Fold in the pecans to serve.

Serves ten to twelve

George Vanderbilt's Birthday

George Vanderbilt celebrated his forty-second birthday in November of 1904 with a ten-course meal for twenty-seven guests. Dinner began with oysters on the half-shell, followed by Consommé Julienne, Halibut with Sauce Hollandaise and Cucumber Salade, and Chicken Mousse with Mushroom Sauce. The main course featured Saddle of Mutton with Currant Jelly and Potatoes with Petit Peas, followed by Pastry Cheese Puffs and another hot course of Virginia Ham and Spinach with Pineapple Salade and crackers. Dessert included ice cream, brandied peaches, and cakes, followed by coffee. The day after this sumptuous dinner, Mr. Vanderbilt noted in the Menu Book, "The dinner last night was very good."

The 1904 Menu Book

Biltmore's 1904 Menu Book documents luncheons and dinners served between September 27 and December 31, 1904. All of the proposed menus are handwritten in ink, although not all were written by the same person. More than eighty were altered in some manner before they were approved. Sometimes a course or menu item was crossed out in pen or pencil and eliminated altogether. At other times, a substitution was added. Occasionally two options were offered and one was declined. The number of guests expected for meals was also noted, usually in Mrs. Vanderbilt's handwriting. A few instructions and comments are in Mr. Vanderbilt's handwriting.

The Biltmore House chef created the above pictured ten-course menu to serve at the celebration of George Vanderbilt's forty-second birthday.
Note the misspelling of "mousse," which the chef records as "mouses"!

Historic Food Production on Biltmore Estate

It was George Vanderbilt's hope that Biltmore Estate would become self-supporting, and he established agricultural operations to produce food for consumption in Biltmore House. Biltmore Farms included the Biltmore Dairy, and its letterhead listed such diverse products as American Jersey Cattle Club cows for milk, cream, and butter, as well as sheep, hogs, poultry, fruits, vegetables, and sourwood honey. At the heart of Biltmore's agricultural success was a commitment to purchasing state-of-the-art equipment and hiring trained specialists who employed the most up-to-date methods available. Vanderbilt was cited in numerous journals and newspaper articles for his support of modern agriculture.

Fall Harvest Creamed Corn

6 ears fresh corn
1 tablespoon butter
1/4 cup finely chopped leek
1 tablespoon chopped shallot
1 teaspoon chopped garlic
1/4 cup Biltmore Chardonnay Sur Lies
2 cups heavy cream
1 tablespoon chopped fresh thyme
salt and freshly ground white pepper to taste

Cut the kernels from the cobs with a chef's knife, discarding the cobs. Melt the butter in a heavy saucepan over medium heat. Add the leek, shallot and garlic and sauté for 2 minutes. Stir in the corn and cook until the corn is tender.

Add the wine, stirring up any of the mixture that has adhered to the bottom of the saucepan. Cook until the wine has evaporated. Add the cream and simmer for 15 to 20 minutes or to the desired consistency, stirring occasionally. Season with the thyme, salt and white pepper. Keep warm until serving time.

Serves four or five

Goat Cheese and Roasted Beet Tarts

2 frozen (5-inch) tart shells
12 baby red beets
3 tablespoons salt
2 quarts water
1¹/2 cups goat cheese, softened
1 teaspoon chopped garlic
1 tablespoon chopped fresh basil
1 tablespoon sliced chives
2 tablespoons chopped fresh thyme
4 ounces arugula
2 tablespoons sherry vinegar
¹/4 cup extra-virgin olive oil
cracked pepper to taste

Preheat the oven to 325 degrees. Remove the tart shells from the wrapper, but leave in the tins. Pierce with a fork and bake for 10 minutes. Cool to room temperature. Reduce the oven temperature to 300 degrees.

Cook the beets with the salt and water in a saucepan until tender. Remove to a paper towel to drain and cool slightly. Remove the skins from the warm beets with the paper towel and slice the beets, reserving the ends for the topping.

Combine the goat cheese with the garlic, basil, chives and thyme in a bowl and mix well. Spread half the mixture in the tart shells, smoothing the tops with a warm knife.

Layer the sliced beets over the goat cheese mixture and sprinkle with the remaining goat cheese mixture. Bake for 5 to 10 minutes or until heated through. Remove the tarts to serving plates. Sprinkle with the arugula. Combine the reserved beet ends with the sherry vinegar in a blender and process until smooth. Add the olive oil gradually, processing constantly at low speed. Drizzle over the tarts and season with pepper.

Serves four to six

Wine Master's Suggestion: Biltmore Viognier

Thanksgiving Dinner, 1904

Thanksgiving dinner in 1904 began with oysters on the half-shell, followed by Consommé Royale, chicken broth garnished with molded and poached bouillon, egg and herbs. Broiled Spanish mackerel and Cucumber Salade came next, followed by Calves' Brains with Mushroom Sauce; Roast Turkey with Cranberry Jelly; Virginia ham with tomatoes and celery; sweet potatoes, peas, and beets. Dessert included mince pie, cakes, and pineapple ice cream, probably frozen in a tall copper mold and garnished with whipped cream and a tuft of leaves cut from a fresh pineapple, infinitely more imaginative than the modern variety scooped from a cardboard container.

Turkey and Dressing

Domesticated turkeys from the Poultry Farm and wild birds from Biltmore's woods found their way to the Banquet Hall via the Rotisserie Kitchen. They also appeared in soups, croquettes, creamed and chipped dishes, and salads. Cook's assistant Ellen Davis prepared roast turkey and dressing for Christmas and Thanksgiving dinners, and her family donated her recipe to Biltmore's archives. The recipe calls for a twenty-five-pound turkey, and the dressing contains a dozen hard-boiled eggs, homemade corn bread, and biscuits. Biltmore's 1904 Menu Book documents that the Vanderbilts dined on turkey once every three days. It may well have been one of Mr. Vanderbilt's favorite foods.

114

Truffled Creamed Spinach

Serve Truffled Creamed Spinach with grilled beef, as a side dish, or even on its own.

1 tablespoon minced garlic
1/2 cup (1 stick) butter, melted
1/2 cup chopped yellow onion
1/2 teaspoon kosher salt
1/8 teaspoon red pepper flakes
1/2 cup all-purpose flour
4 cups milk
1/4 cup heavy cream

1/8 teaspoon nutmeg
1 cup thawed frozen chopped spinach,
    squeezed to remove any excess moisture
1/4 cup (1 ounce) grated Parmesan cheese
1/4 teaspoon Tabasco sauce
11/4 teaspoons truffle oil
1/4 teaspoon black pepper
kosher salt to taste

Sauté the garlic in the butter in a medium saucepan over medium heat for 30 seconds. Add the onion, 1/2 teaspoon kosher salt and the red pepper flakes and sauté for 4 to 5 minutes or until the onion is tender. Add the flour and cook for 3 to 4 minutes, whisking constantly until no lumps remain. Whisk in the milk gradually. Cook until thickened, whisking constantly.

Add the cream and nutmeg. Reduce the heat and simmer for 5 minutes, stirring frequently. Stir in the spinach, Parmesan cheese, Tabasco sauce, truffle oil and black pepper. Season with kosher salt to taste. Serve warm.

Serves six to eight

Mashed Sweet Potatoes with Chipotle Chile and Vanilla

The balance between sweet and hot works well with the sweet potatoes. If a less spicy dish is desired, you can reduce the chipotle chiles to one teaspoon. This is a great dish to serve with Thanksgiving dinner.

21/2 pounds sweet potatoes, peeled
    and chopped
1 tablespoon kosher salt
1/2 cup (1 stick) butter
2 teaspoons minced chipotle chile
1/2 cup sugar

1/4 teaspoon cinnamon
1 teaspoon vanilla extract
1/4 cup heavy cream
1 tablespoon orange juice
1 teaspoon kosher salt

Fill a medium saucepan halfway with cold water and add the sweet potatoes and 1 tablespoon kosher salt. Bring to a boil and reduce the heat. Simmer until the sweet potatoes are fork-tender. Drain the sweet potatoes and return to the saucepan. Mash just until a few lumps remain; do not overmash.

Add the butter, chipotle chile, sugar, cinnamon and vanilla and mix well with a rubber spatula. Add the cream, orange juice and 1 teaspoon kosher salt; mix gently. Serve warm.

Serves six to eight

Wine Master's Suggestion: Biltmore Dry Riesling

Corn and Cheddar Biscuits

1/3 cup cornmeal
3/4 cup all-purpose flour
1/2 cup cake flour
1 tablespoon sugar
1 1/2 teaspoons baking powder
1/8 teaspoon baking soda
1/2 teaspoon kosher salt
1/4 cup vegetable shortening
1/2 bunch green onions, chopped
3/4 cup frozen corn, thawed
3/4 cup (3 ounces) shredded
   Cheddar cheese
1 cup buttermilk
1/2 cup (1 stick) butter, melted

Preheat the oven to 400 degrees. Combine the cornmeal, all-purpose flour, sugar, cake flour, baking powder, baking soda and kosher salt in a large mixing bowl. Mix in the shortening with your fingers until incorporated. Add the green onions, corn and Cheddar cheese and mix well with your fingers. Add the buttermilk and stir lightly just until mixed; do not overmix.

Place on a floured surface and pat 3/4 inch thick. Cut with a 2- to 2 1/2-inch biscuit cutter, dipping the cutter in additional flour before each cut. Place close together but not touching on a baking parchment-lined baking sheet. Brush with some of the butter. Bake for 20 minutes or until golden brown. Brush again with the remaining butter.

Makes one dozen

The Fall Fair

Estate workers and their families celebrated the harvest with a Fall Fair, held on the hill behind the Horse Barn. The annual event included competitions for the best fresh fruits and vegetables, canned goods, baked goods, and needlework. Edith Vanderbilt served as a judge, handing out highly coveted blue, red, and white ribbons to the winners. After the judging, everyone enjoyed Biltmore Dairy ice cream. Departmental teams competed in softball games and tugs-of-war for prizes. Other competitions included catching a greased pig and climbing a greased pole. The festivities concluded with a square dance, with estate musicians and callers providing the music and direction.

Baker's Butter Rolls

3 cups bread flour
1/4 cup sugar
2 teaspoons instant dry yeast
1 teaspoon kosher salt
3 eggs
1/3 cup milk
1 cup (2 sticks) unsalted butter, softened

Combine the flour, sugar, yeast and kosher salt in a mixing bowl. Add the eggs and milk and mix with a dough hook at low speed until the mixture forms a ball and pulls from the side of the bowl. Increase the speed to medium and mix for 2 minutes. Add the butter gradually, mixing well until smooth and elastic. Let rise, covered, in the refrigerator for 8 hours to 2 days.

Shape the dough into 24 even balls and place on a baking parchment-lined baking sheet. Let rise at room temperature for 1 1/2 to 2 hours or until almost doubled in bulk.

Preheat the oven to 325 degrees. Bake the rolls for 12 to 15 minutes or until golden brown.

Makes two dozen

Chrysanthemum peruvianum

Praline Cheesecake

Our Praline Cheesecake has a decidedly southern flair. The addition of brown sugar, pecans, and caramel gives it a distinctive flavor that pays homage to the ever-popular Louisiana praline. The water bath ensures a slow and even baking.

20 ounces cream cheese, softened
1 cup packed brown sugar
4 teaspoons cinnamon
2 teaspoons vanilla extract
1/3 cup sour cream

1/2 cup prepared caramel sauce
4 eggs, lightly beaten
1 cup chopped pecans
1 Graham Cracker Crust (below)

Preheat the oven to 300 degrees. Combine the cream cheese, brown sugar, cinnamon and vanilla in a mixing bowl. Beat with a paddle attachment at medium speed until smooth, scraping the bowl frequently. Beat in the sour cream and caramel sauce and scrape the bowl. Add the eggs gradually, beating constantly and scraping the bowl halfway through. Mix in the pecans.

Spread the mixture evenly in the Graham Cracker Crust. Place the pan in a larger pan and add enough hot water to reach halfway up the side of the cheesecake pan. Bake for 1 1/2 hours or until the cheesecake is set in the center. Cool in the pan on a wire rack for 1 hour. Invert onto a plate, tapping lightly if necessary to release. Remove the baking parchment and invert onto a serving plate. Chill until serving time.

You can prepare this in a springform pan, but be sure to wrap the pan in foil to prevent the water from the water bath from seeping into the pan. Use an ovenproof pan large enough to hold hot water reaching halfway up the side of the cheesecake pan and maintain the water level thoughout the baking process.

Serves twelve

Wine Master's Suggestion: Biltmore Century

Graham Cracker Crust

1 1/2 cups graham cracker crumbs
1/2 cup sugar
1/4 cup (1/2 stick) butter, melted

Spray a 9- or 10-inch round baking pan with nonstick cooking spray and line the bottom with baking parchment. Combine the graham cracker crumbs and sugar in a bowl. Add the butter and mix well. Press over the bottom of the prepared pan.

Makes one crust

Apple Tart

Tart Pastry
1/2 cup (1 stick) unsalted butter,
  softened
1/4 cup sugar
pinch of salt
1/2 teaspoon vanilla extract
1 egg, lightly beaten
1 1/2 cups all-purpose flour

Streusel Topping
1 cup all-purpose flour
1/2 cup packed brown sugar
1/4 cup (1/2 stick) butter, melted

Tart
4 or 5 Granny Smith apples,
  peeled, cored and thinly sliced
1/4 cup sugar
1 teaspoon cinnamon
1/2 teaspoon ground nutmeg
1/4 teaspoon ground cloves

Garnish
sliced dried figs

For the tart pastry, combine the butter, sugar, salt and vanilla in a mixing bowl. Cream with a paddle attachment until light and fluffy. Beat in the egg and scrape the side of the bowl. Add the flour gradually, mixing until incorporated. Shape into a disk. Wrap in plastic wrap and chill in the refrigerator for 2 to 8 hours.

For the topping, mix the flour and brown sugar in a small bowl. Add the butter and work with your fingers until smooth. Chill in the refrigerator for 2 hours.

For the tart, preheat the oven to 350 degrees. Toss the apples with the sugar, cinnamon, nutmeg and cloves in a bowl.

Spray a tart pan with a removable bottom with nonstick cooking spray. Roll the tart pastry 1/4 inch thick on a lightly floured surface. Place in the prepared pan, pressing into the bottom and trimming excess dough. Spoon the apple mixture into the tart shell and sprinkle with the topping.

Bake for 25 to 35 minutes or until golden brown. Cool in the pan on a wire rack for 10 minutes. Remove to a serving plate and garnish with figs. Serve warm with whipped cream or vanilla ice cream.

Serves six to eight

Wine Master's Suggestion:
Biltmore Methode Champenoise Pas de Deux Sec

Field to Table Fruit and Vegetable Cultivation

The cultivation of fruits and vegetables for Biltmore's Field to Table program is modeled on George Vanderbilt's Market Garden. The Kitchen Garden, located near the Historic Horse Barn, produces soft fruits, vegetables, and herbs for estate restaurants. It includes five and one-half acres of fruit and vegetable production and several additional acres of pasture.

A one-acre interactive educational plot features herbs, small fruits, cereal grains, and vegetables grown in themed beds, as well as traditional home garden plantings. Today's gardeners apply Integrated Pest Management principles, which include crop rotation, cover cropping, composting, mulching, selecting disease-resistant crops, and attracting beneficial insects.

Pecan Pie

There is nothing more traditionally southern than pecan pie. Pecan trees are native to the southern United States, so they were readily available to the cook. Exactly where the original recipe was developed is still a mystery, but no one can deny its rightful place on the southern table.

3/4 cup packed brown sugar
3/4 cup granulated sugar
1/2 cup corn syrup
2 tablespoons cake flour
1 teaspoon salt
2 tablespoons unsalted butter, melted
5 eggs, lightly beaten
2 cups chopped pecans
1 unbaked (9-inch) pie shell

Preheat the oven to 350 degrees. Combine the brown sugar, granulated sugar and corn syrup in a mixing bowl and beat with a paddle attachment until smooth. Add the flour and salt and mix well. Beat in the melted butter and then add the eggs gradually, scraping the bowl frequently.

Sprinkle the pecans in the pie shell. Spread the filling over the pecans. Bake for 40 to 50 minutes or until the filling is set and the crust is golden brown. Cool on a wire rack. Serve with whipped cream.

Serves six to eight

Wine Master's Suggestion:
Biltmore Winemaker's
Selection Chenin Blanc

Narcissus autumnalis

Sweet Potato Crunch Pie

Our very own Carolina sweet potatoes grace this sumptuous pie. We have also incorporated another southern favorite by topping it with a crunchy pecan topping. Because sweet potatoes are one of the most nutritious vegetables around, you can feel good while enjoying this treat.

Pecan Crunch Topping
1 cup all-purpose flour
1/2 cup packed brown sugar
1 cup chopped pecans
1/4 cup (1/2 stick) butter, melted

Pie
1 1/2 pounds sweet potatoes, peeled and chopped
1/3 cup packed brown sugar
1 cup plus 2 tablespoons granulated sugar
1 tablespoon heavy cream
1 tablespoon vanilla extract
1 tablespoon salt
2 eggs, lightly beaten
1 unbaked (9-inch) pie shell

For the topping, mix the flour, brown sugar and pecans in a small bowl. Add the butter and mix with your fingers until incorporated. Spread the mixture on a baking sheet and chill until the butter is firm. Chop slightly.

For the pie, preheat the oven to 350 degrees. Steam the sweet potatoes for 20 to 30 minutes or until fork-tender. Place in a mixing bowl and mash with a paddle attachment at medium speed. Add the brown sugar and granulated sugar to the hot sweet potatoes and mix until smooth and slightly cooled. Add the cream, vanilla and salt and mix well. Beat in the eggs.

Spread the mixture in the pie shell and sprinkle with the topping. Bake for 35 to 40 minutes or until set. Cool on a wire rack and store in the refrigerator until serving time. Serve with whipped cream or vanilla ice cream.

Serves six to eight

We All Scream for Ice Cream

Biltmore Dairy ice cream was the stuff of legend. By 1896, the Dairy had become a popular attraction of estate visitors, who were allowed to sample the milk. Estate children enjoyed ice cream every Sunday afternoon, when they could have it free. Mildred Buchanan's brother worked in the Creamery. Mildred went to see him every day after school and "would look at him real pitiful" until he gave her some butter pecan ice cream. Virtually every estate get-together included ice cream from the Dairy. Ruby Redmon couldn't remember a gathering at which her family didn't serve it.

Pumpkin Ice Cream

2¹/2 cups heavy cream
1 cup half-and-half
¹/2 cup sugar
6 egg yolks, beaten
3/4 cup solid-pack pumpkin purée

Combine the cream, half-and-half and sugar in a saucepan. Bring just to a simmer to scald. Whisk a small amount of the hot liquid into the beaten egg yolks, then beat the egg yolks into the hot liquid. Cook until the mixture begins to thicken, stirring constantly. Whisk in the pumpkin purée. Spoon into an ice cream freezer container and freeze using the manufacturer's instructions.

Makes one and one-half quarts

Wine Master's Suggestion: Biltmore Dry Riesling

Biltmore Hot Chocolate with Homemade Marshmallows

1/4 cup baking cocoa
1/2 cup sugar
1/4 teaspoon cinnamon
4 cups milk
1/4 teaspoon vanilla extract
Homemade Marshmallows (below)

Combine the baking cocoa, sugar and cinnamon in a saucepan. Stir in the milk and vanilla and heat just to serving temperature. Ladle into mugs and top with Homemade Marshmallows.

Serves four to six

Homemade Marshmallows

1/2 cup corn syrup
1 1/2 cups sugar
1/2 cup water
4 egg whites
2 tablespoons unflavored gelatin
1/4 cup cold water
1/2 teaspoon vanilla extract

Combine the corn syrup and sugar with 1/2 cup water in a saucepan and bring to a boil. Boil to the soft-ball stage, or 225 degrees on a candy thermometer.

Beat the egg whites at medium speed in a mixing bowl until soft peaks form. Sprinkle the gelatin over 1/4 cup cold water in a bowl and let stand to soften.

Remove the corn syrup mixture from the heat and add the gelatin, stirring to dissolve completely. Pour gradually over the egg whites, beating constantly at medium speed. Add the vanilla and beat until stiff, increasing the speed if necessary but taking care not to overbeat.

Sprinkle your hands lightly with cornstarch and pat the mixture evenly over a baking sheet dusted with cornstarch. Let stand until dry and cool. Cut to the desired size with a cookie cutter dusted with cornstarch.

Serves four to six

As early as 1895,

the house buzzed throughout the

holiday season with preparations

for company; the home was

fully occupied, the train station was a

hub of activity, and loved ones were

greeted eagerly by the Vanderbilts,

who offered plans for a

winter retreat in the mountains.

Winter

Winter

in the mountains. Chefs in the kitchens of Biltmore House undoubtedly drew upon the root vegetables plentiful in the Appalachians—sweet potatoes, parsnips, turnips, beets—and raided the swollen pantries brimming with sweets and foodstuffs, jellies and preserves, and Mason jars filled with the summer's bounty.

Biltmore has always been about family and friends, especially when they've gathered around the table to share one another's company. As early as 1895, the house buzzed throughout the holiday season with preparations for company; the home was fully occupied, the train station was a hub of activity, and loved ones were greeted eagerly by the Vanderbilts, who offered plans for a winter retreat

The smoked meats and roasted game from the rotisserie filled the upper floors with the smell of

applewood and hickory, and the pastry chefs sifted and stirred, punctuating the air with a heady mixture

of scents: freshly baked yeast bread, sweet molasses, and cinnamon. Simmering stews and fragrant soups

bubbled on the stovetop in the main kitchen, and house staff busily polished silver, washed dishes, and

brought out freshly laundered linens, ensuring that houseguests and their servants were afforded every

comfort. The entire house was in motion as the Vanderbilts and their guests gathered in the Tapestry

Gallery for a fireside afternoon tea, transported a basket of warm scones for a morning carriage ride, or sat

down to an elegant ten-course meal beneath the boughs of the towering Christmas tree in the Banquet Hall.

Winter Brunch Menu

Homemade Cinnamon Rolls

Pumpkin Pancakes with
Toasted Pecan Butter

Creamed Chipped Beef with
Peppered Challah Toast

Maine Lobster Frittata with
Trout Caviar

Vanilla Pear Mimosa

Maine Lobster Frittata with Trout Caviar

Nut-Crusted Brie with Cherry Chutney

1 cup almonds, lightly crushed
1/4 cup pecans, lightly crushed
1/4 cup walnuts, lightly crushed
1 (2-pound) wheel Brie cheese
3 eggs, lightly beaten
1 cup heavy cream
Cherry Chutney (below)

Preheat the oven to 350 degrees. Mix the almonds, pecans and walnuts in a small bowl. Cut the Brie cheese into the desired portions. Whisk the eggs and cream together in a bowl. Dip the cheese into the egg mixture and coat with the nuts. Place in a baking pan and bake until the cheese is softened and the nuts are golden brown.

Place the cheese on heated plates. Spoon Cherry Chutney over the cheese and around the edges of the plates. Serve with slices of toasted French baguette.

Serves six

Wine Master's Suggestion:
Biltmore Methode Champenoise Blanc de Noir Brut

Cherry Chutney

1 pound dried cherries
2 cups orange juice
2 tablespoons red wine vinegar
1/2 cup grated ginger
1 teaspoon whole coriander seeds
1 1/4 cups sugar

Combine the dried cherries with the orange juice and vinegar in a saucepan. Add the ginger, coriander seeds and sugar and mix well. Bring to a boil and reduce the heat. Cook to a syrupy consistency, stirring constantly.

Serves four to six

Artichoke Dip

1/2 cup (1 stick) unsalted butter
1 fennel bulb, finely chopped
3 shallots, minced
2 garlic cloves, minced
2 (15-ounce) cans artichoke hearts,
   drained and chopped
1 cup all-purpose flour
1 cup Biltmore Château Reserve Chardonnay
2 cups milk
4 cups heavy cream
3 tablespoons chopped fresh basil
3 tablespoons chopped fresh oregano
6 tablespoons chopped Italian parsley
8 dashes Tabasco sauce, or to taste
4 teaspoons kosher salt
2 teaspoons freshly ground white pepper
1 1/4 cups (5 ounces) grated Parmesan cheese

Garnish
chopped fresh basil, oregano and parsley

Melt the butter in a heavy saucepan over medium heat and cook until frothy. Add the fennel, shallots and garlic and sauté until translucent. Add the artichoke hearts and sauté for 2 minutes. Add the flour and cook for 2 minutes or until a nutty aroma develops, stirring constantly.

Add the wine, stirring to deglaze the skillet. Cook until the aroma of alcohol is no longer detected, stirring constantly. Add the milk and cream and simmer until thickened, stirring constantly. Stir in the basil, oregano, parsley, Tabasco sauce, kosher salt and white pepper.

Spoon into ramekins or ovenproof bowls and sprinkle with Parmesan cheese. Broil just until the tops are golden brown. Garnish with additional fresh herbs and serve with sourdough bread or grilled pita points.

Serves six

Polenta Gateau with Olives and Red Bell Peppers

2 red bell peppers
1 tablespoon olive oil
2 ounces basil leaves
1 tablespoon olive oil
1 cup pitted kalamata olives
3 quarts (12 cups) water

1 1/2 cups (3 sticks) butter
1 tablespoon white pepper
2 cups heavy cream
3 tablespoons salt
4 cups uncooked polenta
3 cups (12 ounces) grated Parmesan cheese

Preheat the oven to 375 degrees. Brush the red bell peppers with 1 tablespoon olive oil and place on a baking sheet. Roast for 10 minutes. Place in a plastic bag and seal; let stand for 5 minutes to loosen the skins. Slip off and discard the skins and remove the seeds. Purée the bell peppers in a blender. Purée the basil leaves with 1 tablespoon olive oil in a blender. Purée the olives separately in a blender. Reserve the purées in separate containers.

Bring the water, butter and white pepper to a boil in a saucepan. Add the cream and salt and return to a boil. Stir in the polenta gradually. Reduce the heat to medium-low and cook for 25 to 30 minutes, stirring frequently. Stir in half the Parmesan cheese.

Divide the polenta into 3 portions in separate bowls. Add the red pepper purée to 1 portion, the basil purée to 1 portion and the olive purée to 1 portion.

Spray a deep baking pan with nonstick cooking spray and sprinkle with the remaining Parmesan cheese. Bake for 5 minutes or just until the cheese is golden brown. Spread the roasted red pepper polenta in the prepared pan. Chill in the refrigerator until partially set. Repeat the process with the basil polenta and the olive polenta. Chill for 12 hours before serving. Invert the gateau on a serving plate and cut into wedges to serve.

Serves four to six

Wine Master's Suggestion:
Biltmore Sangiovese

Arugula and Endive Salad with Vanilla-Roasted Pears and Blue Cheese

Vanilla-Roasted Pears
1 cup sugar
1 cup water
1 vanilla bean, split
1/4 cup apple juice
1 tablespoon Champagne vinegar
2 Bartlett pears

Salad
8 ounces arugula
2 heads Belgian endive, split and sliced
1 1/2 cups (6 ounces) crumbled Clemson
   blue cheese
salt and cracked pepper to taste
Champagne Vinaigrette (below)

For the pears, preheat the oven to 275 degrees. Combine the sugar, water and vanilla bean in a saucepan. Simmer for 10 to 15 minutes or until syrupy. Add the apple juice and vinegar and simmer for 5 minutes.

Peel the pears and cut into halves lengthwise. Place in a deep baking dish and pour the apple juice mixture over the top. Cover with foil and roast for 1 hour or until tender, basting after 30 minutes. Cool to room temperature. Drain, reserving the cooking liquid and removing the vanilla bean. Slice the pears as desired.

For the salad, combine the arugula, endive and blue cheese in a salad bowl. Sprinkle with salt and pepper. Add the pears and the desired amount of Champagne Vinaigrette and toss to coat well. Spoon onto salad plates and drizzle with the reserved cooking liquid if desired for additional sweetness.

Serves four

Wine Master's Suggestion: Biltmore Dry Riesling

Champagne Vinaigrette

3 tablespoons Champagne vinegar
1 teaspoon minced shallot
2 tablespoons honey
1 teaspoon Dijon mustard

1/2 cup plus 1 tablespoon vegetable oil
salt and freshly ground white pepper
   to taste

Combine the vinegar, shallot, honey and Dijon mustard in a blender. Add the oil gradually, processing constantly at low speed until thickened. Season with salt and white pepper. Pour into a container with a spout and chill until serving time.

Serves four

Cauliflower Vichyssoise

florets of 1 head cauliflower
2 Idaho potatoes, peeled and chopped
1/2 cup chopped white onion
1/2 cup chopped leek
1/4 cup chopped fennel bulb

5 or 6 garlic cloves, chopped
5 cups heavy cream
salt and freshly ground white pepper
   to taste

Combine the cauliflower, potatoes, onion, leek, fennel and garlic in a saucepan. Add the cream and simmer for 15 to 20 minutes or until the vegetables are tender. Season with salt and white pepper. Pour into a blender and process until smooth. Strain back into the saucepan and bring to a simmer. Adjust the seasonings and ladle into soup bowls.

Serves four to six

Country Chicken Soup

This is a perennial favorite at the Stable Café.

2 cups chopped onions
1 1/2 cups chopped celery
1 1/2 cups chopped carrots
3 tablespoons olive oil
3 pounds chicken, chopped

3 cups drained black-eyed peas
3 quarts (12 cups) chicken bouillon
2 tablespoons rubbed sage
12 ounces frozen chopped spinach, thawed
salt and pepper to taste

Sauté the onions, celery and carrots in the olive oil in a 3-gallon saucepan or Dutch oven over medium heat until the onions are translucent. Add the chicken, peas, chicken bouillon and sage and bring to a boil. Reduce the heat and simmer for 30 minutes, stirring occasionally. Add the spinach and season with salt and pepper. Cook until heated through and ladle into soup bowls.

Serves twelve

Wine Master's Suggestion: Biltmore Cabernet Sauvignon

Braised Button Mushroom Soup with Truffled Crème Fraîche

1¼ cups chopped shallots
¼ cup chopped garlic
1 cup (2 sticks) butter, melted
2 pounds button mushrooms
1 cup Biltmore Château Reserve
    Chardonnay
1 gallon (16 cups) chicken stock

2 bay leaves
2 tablespoons chopped fresh thyme
2 tablespoons salt
1½ teaspoons pepper
½ cup crème fraîche
2 tablespoons white truffle oil

Sauté the shallots and garlic in the butter in a saucepan over medium heat until tender. Add the mushrooms and sauté for 5 minutes. Add the wine, stirring to deglaze the saucepan. Cook until the liquid evaporates. Stir in the chicken stock, bay leaves and thyme.

Simmer for 30 minutes. Season with the salt and pepper and discard the bay leaves. Ladle into soup bowls and top with a dollop of crème fraîche and a drizzle of truffle oil.

Serves eight   *Wine Master's Suggestion*: Biltmore Château Reserve Chardonnay

Truffled Potato and Leek Soup

2 yellow onions, chopped
2 fennel bulbs, chopped
1 leek, chopped
3 garlic cloves, minced
½ cup (1 stick) butter
1 cup all-purpose flour
2 cups Biltmore Château Reserve
    Chardonnay
4 Idaho potatoes, peeled and chopped
½ gallon (8 cups) chicken stock or
    chicken broth
2 cups milk

1½ cups half-and-half
1½ cups heavy cream
grated zest and juice of 2 lemons
1 tablespoon chopped fresh thyme
1 teaspoon grated nutmeg
3 tablespoons kosher salt
2 teaspoons pepper
1 tablespoon white truffle oil

Garnish
chopped fresh herbs and toasted bread

Sauté the onions, fennel, leek and garlic in the butter in a saucepan until the onions are tender and translucent. Add the flour and cook for 1 minute, stirring constantly. Add the wine, stirring to deglaze the saucepan. Cook until reduced by ¾.

Add the potatoes, chicken stock, milk, half-and-half and cream. Bring just to a boil and reduce the heat. Simmer for 30 minutes.

Add the lemon zest, lemon juice, thyme, nutmeg, kosher salt and pepper. Purée with an immersion blender or in a food processor. Ladle into heated soup bowls and drizzle with the truffle oil. Garnish with fresh herbs and toasted bread.

Serves six

Favorite Foods

The 1904 Menu Book documents that Mr. Vanderbilt liked fried
ham and eggs or shirred (baked) eggs and bacon for breakfast. When he
requested that some of the ham that was broiled for lunch also be
served cold, it reappeared the following day with salad. When he asked for
purée of parsnips as a vegetable, it appeared in three menus the
following week. He also preferred lamb chops when rabbit was served.
He noted on one luncheon menu: "Iced pudding last night was too
cold—take it off ice a little while before dinner when serving it again."

Mrs. Vanderbilt spent many hours on Biltmore Estate visiting farm and dairy
families, bringing food or maternity baskets, giving away Cornelia's
outgrown clothing, and handing out flower seeds. Ruby Gaddy recalled that
women baked cakes when they knew she was coming, and numerous
oral history accounts mention that she tasted all the cakes at the Fall Fair.
And what dinner dessert was served most frequently according to
Biltmore's Menu Book? Cake! The Vanderbilts usually had cake every
third night; this statistic does not take into account pastries
and other desserts classified as cakes at the turn of the last century.

Afternoon Tea, 1900

The Vanderbilts adopted the time-honored English upper-class practice
of taking afternoon tea and often gathered on the Loggia for afternoon tea
during house parties. This photograph was taken during a house party
to celebrate the recent birth of baby Cornelia. Those pictured are, left to right:
Edith Vanderbilt, Mademoiselle Marie Rambaud (Edith's former chaperone),
Lila Vanderbilt Webb (George's sister), Effie Caesar (George's cousin),
an unidentified man and woman, and George Vanderbilt.

Grilled Filet Mignon with Fingerling Potato Gratin and Syrah Glacé

Fingerling Potato Gratin
8 ounces bacon, cut into thin strips
8 ounces pearl onions
1 1/2 pounds fingerling potatoes, cooked
4 ounces crumbled Gorgonzola cheese
salt and pepper to taste

Filet Mignon
6 (6-ounce) filets mignons
salt and pepper to taste
olive oil
Syrah Glacé (below)

For the gratin, preheat the oven to 350 degrees. Cook the bacon in a hot skillet until crisp and brown. Remove the bacon with a slotted spoon and add the pearl onions to the pan drippings. Reduce the heat and cook until the onions are caramelized.

Combine the bacon, pearl onions, potatoes and Gorgonzola cheese in a bowl and mix gently. Season lightly with salt and pepper, taking care not to oversalt, as the bacon and cheese are salty. Spoon into a buttered baking dish and bake until the cheese melts and the potatoes are heated through. Keep warm.

For the filets mignons, preheat a charcoal or gas grill to medium. Season the steaks with salt and pepper and brush with olive oil. Grill for 2 minutes on each side for medium-rare or until done to taste.

To serve, spoon the gratin onto serving plates and top with a filet mignon. Ladle the Syrah Glacé around and on the filets.

Serves six

Wine Master's Suggestion: Biltmore Antler Hill Cabernet Sauvignon

Syrah Glacé

2 cups minced shallots
1/4 cup minced garlic
3 thyme sprigs
2 bay leaves
olive oil
1 bottle Biltmore Signature North Coast Syrah
2 cups beef broth or veal stock
2 tablespoons butter
salt and pepper to taste

Sauté the shallots, garlic, thyme and bay leaves lightly in a small amount of olive oil in a heated saucepan. Add the wine and bring to a boil. Reduce the heat and simmer until the mixture is reduced by 3/4. Add the beef broth and cook until reduced to 2 cups. Strain the mixture, discarding the solids. Return to the heat and add the butter gradually. Season with salt and pepper.

Serves six

Field to Table Livestock Program

Biltmore's Field to Table livestock program is modeled on George Vanderbilt's animal husbandry operations at the turn of the last century. Purebred Angus and Limousin herds include 250 mature females, 5 breeding bulls, 240 calves, 60 yearling steers, and 50 yearling replacement heifers. Sheep herds include purebred Dorsets and South African Dorpers, with 100 breeding females, 5 rams, 20 replacement yearling ewes, and 150 lambs. Biltmore beef and lamb are humanely raised in pastures and fed natural grains and forages. No antibiotics are used in their feeds, nor are hormone implants employed.

The Farms on Biltmore Estate

Purebred livestock at the turn of the last century included Jersey cows at the Dairy, Berkshire hogs at the Pig Farm, and many breeds of chickens, turkeys, and other fowl at the Poultry Farm, all on the East Side of the French Broad River. English Southdowns were raised at the Sheep Farm on the West Side. These livestock operations provided eggs, poultry, meat, and dairy products for Biltmore House, as well as for sale in the community. Supporting operations included a veterinarian, butcher's shop, repair shop, smithy, and two river ferries. Many farm and dairy workers and their families lived on Biltmore Estate.

Beef Bourguignonne

The Stable Café's version of the classic French beef stew is accented with port and shiitake mushrooms.

Port Marinade
1 cup ruby port
3 cups Biltmore Cabernet Sauvignon
4 shallots, coarsely chopped
6 garlic cloves, coarsely chopped
1 tablespoon chopped fresh thyme
1 teaspoon coarsely ground pepper

Beef
3 1/2 pounds beef chuck, trimmed and cut into
    3/4-inch cubes
salt and pepper to taste
1/2 cup olive oil
1/2 cup pearl onions
1/4 cup all-purpose flour
1 pound shiitake mushrooms
6 bay leaves
2 cups beef stock, heated

For the marinade, combine the port, cabernet, shallots, garlic, thyme and pepper in a bowl and mix well.

For the beef, add the beef cubes to the marinade and coat well. Marinate, covered, in the refrigerator for 8 hours or longer. Drain, reserving the marinade. Separate the beef from the marinated shallots and garlic, reserving the vegetables separately.

Season the beef with salt and pepper. Sauté in 2 batches in the heated olive oil in a large Dutch oven or saucepan over medium-high heat until brown. Remove the beef to a bowl with a slotted spoon. Add the reserved marinated vegetables and pearl onions to the drippings in the Dutch oven and sauté until light brown. Add the flour. Cook for 1 minute, stirring constantly. Add the mushrooms and beef.

Add the reserved marinade and bay leaves. Bring to a boil and reduce the heat. Simmer for 30 minutes. Add the beef stock and simmer for 1 hour or until the beef is tender and the liquid is reduced and thickened to the desired consistency. Season with salt and pepper and discard the bay leaves.

Serves four to six   *Wine Master's Suggestion*: Biltmore Cabernet Sauvignon

Creamed Chipped Beef with Peppered Challah Toast

This is a new variation of an old classic. The toasted challah creates a good contrast of texture with the creamed chipped beef. Challah is an egg yolk-enriched yeast bread with Jewish origins.

Creamed Chipped Beef
1/2 cup (1 stick) butter
6 tablespoons all-purpose flour
6 cups half-and-half
1 yellow onion, cut into halves
dash of Tabasco sauce
pinch of nutmeg
1 teaspoon kosher salt
1/2 teaspoon finely ground pepper
10 ounces corned beef, sliced and chopped

Peppered Challah Toast
1 cup (2 sticks) butter
20 (1-inch) slices challah
coarsely ground pepper to taste

For the chipped beef, melt the butter in a saucepan. Stir in the flour. Cook over low heat for 4 minutes to form a roux, stirring constantly.

Combine the half-and-half with the onion in a saucepan. Cook over low heat for 10 minutes. Remove the onion. Ladle about 1 cup of the half-and-half into the roux, whisking constantly until smooth. Whisk back into the remaining half-and-half in the saucepan. Bring to a simmer and cook until reduced by 1/4, stirring frequently. Stir in the Tabasco sauce, nutmeg, kosher salt and pepper. Add the corned beef and mix well. Simmer for 5 minutes; keep warm.

For the toast, preheat the oven to 350 degrees. Melt the butter in a small saucepan. Brush on both sides of the challah slices and sprinkle with pepper. Arrange on a baking sheet and bake for 5 to 8 minutes or until golden brown.

To serve, place the toasted challah on serving plates and ladle the chipped beef over the bread.

Serves eight to ten

Wine Master's Suggestion: Biltmore Cardinal's Crest

Braised Veal Cheek Cannelloni with Collard Greens

2 pounds veal cheeks
salt and pepper to taste
1/4 cup olive oil
1/4 cup chopped onion
1/4 cup chopped carrots
1/4 cup chopped celery
1/4 cup chopped fennel
3 tablespoons minced garlic
2 tablespoons tomato paste
1 cup Biltmore Cardinal's Crest
2 quarts (8 cups) chicken broth

8 thyme sprigs
1 bay leaf
2 tablespoons roasted garlic
olive oil for sautéing
1/2 cup blanched spinach
1/4 cup blanched basil
1/4 cup (1 ounce) grated Parmesan cheese
6 sheets French pastry dough (feuille de brik), or 6 blanched won ton wrappers
Collard Greens (below)

Preheat the oven to 300 degrees. Remove all fat and silver skin from the veal and season the veal with salt and pepper. Sear in 1/4 cup heated olive oil in a heavy Dutch oven over medium heat, turning every 2 minutes to brown evenly. Remove to a bowl.

Add the onion, carrots, celery, fennel and 3 tablespoons garlic to the drippings in the Dutch oven. Sauté for 6 to 8 minutes or until the vegetables are caramelized. Stir in the tomato paste. Add the wine, stirring to deglaze the Dutch oven and cook until reduced by 3/4.

Return the veal to the Dutch oven and add the chicken broth, thyme and bay leaf. Bring to a simmer and cover. Braise in the oven for 2 1/2 hours or until the veal is very tender. Remove the veal with a slotted spoon and cut into strips, reserving the cooking sauce. Increase the oven temperature to 400 degrees.

Sauté 2 tablespoons roasted garlic in a small amount of olive oil in a small saucepan; drain. Wrap the spinach and basil in a kitchen towel and twist to remove the liquid. Combine with the roasted garlic in a food processor and purée. Season with salt and pepper and stir in the Parmesan cheese. Spoon into a piping bag.

Cut the dough into 3×3-inch pieces and pipe the spinach mixture onto the dough. Top with the veal and roll tightly to enclose the filling, brushing the edges and ends with water or beaten egg and pressing to seal. Arrange on a nonstick baking sheet. Bake for 6 to 8 minutes or until the cannelloni are cooked.

To serve, spoon a small amount of Collard Greens onto serving plates and top with the cannellonis. Serve with the reserved veal cooking sauce.

Serves four to six

Wine Master's Suggestion: Biltmore Red Century

Collard Greens

2 bunches collard greens
8 slices bacon, chopped
1/4 cup chopped onion
2 tablespoons sherry vinegar

1 cup chicken broth
salt and freshly ground white pepper to taste

Chop the collard greens into 1/2-inch pieces. Sauté the bacon in a heavy sauté pan over medium heat until the drippings are rendered. Add the onion and sauté for 3 to 4 minutes or until tender. Add the collard greens and sauté for 4 to 5 minutes. Stir in the vinegar and cook for 3 minutes. Add the chicken broth and cook over low heat for 10 to 15 minutes or until the liquid has evaporated. Season with salt and white pepper.

Serves four to six

Chorizo Bread Pudding with White Cheddar Cheese and Scallions

Serve this for breakfast or brunch. The croissants used in the recipe are the same as you would buy in a bakery, just half the size. They help to create a moister bread pudding. If croissants are not available, you can use French bread or foccacia.

1 tablespoon canola oil
8 ounces chorizo
1/2 cup chopped yellow onion
1/3 cup chopped red bell pepper
1 tablespoon minced garlic
1 teaspoon ground cumin
8 miniature butter croissants, cubed
2 cups (8 ounces) shredded white Cheddar cheese
1/4 cup (1 ounce) grated Parmesan cheese
1/2 cup thinly sliced scallions
1 tablespoon sugar
1/2 teaspoon red pepper flakes
2 teaspoons kosher salt
1/2 teaspoon black pepper
6 eggs, beaten
2 cups milk
2 tablespoons butter, melted

Heat a medium skillet over medium-high heat. Add the canola oil and chorizo and cook until the sausage begins to brown, breaking it up with a spatula. Add the onion, bell pepper, garlic and cumin and sauté for 3 to 4 minutes or until the vegetables are tender. Drain well and cool to room temperature.

Preheat the oven to 325 degrees. Combine the croissants, white Cheddar cheese, Parmesan cheese, scallions, sugar, red pepper flakes, kosher salt and black pepper in a bowl. Add the chorizo mixture and toss to mix well.

Combine the eggs and milk in a mixing bowl and mix well. Add to the sausage mixture with the butter and mix well with a rubber spatula. Spread in a buttered medium baking dish and smooth the top. Place in a larger pan of hot water and bake for 30 to 35 minutes or until set in the center. Serve warm.

Serves six to eight

Coriander-Crusted Pork Tenderloin

1/2 cup bread crumbs
1 tablespoon garlic powder
1 tablespoon onion powder
1/4 cup freshly ground coriander seeds
2 tablespoons freshly ground
   mustard seeds
1/4 cup salt
2 tablespoons freshly ground pepper

1/4 cup (1/2 stick) butter, melted
   and clarified
1 (2-pound) pork tenderloin
2 tablespoons salt
2 teaspoons white pepper
1/4 cup vegetable oil
Chipotle Honey Sweet Potatoes (below)
Brandied Grape Sauce (page 149)

Preheat the oven to 350 degrees. Combine the bread crumbs with the garlic powder, onion powder, coriander, mustard, 1/4 cup salt and 2 tablespoons ground pepper in a large bowl. Add the butter and mix well.

Season the pork with 2 tablespoons salt and 2 teaspoons white pepper. Coat with the bread crumb mixture. Heat the vegetable oil in a large skillet. Add the pork and sear on all sides. Place in a roasting pan and roast for 15 minutes for medium well or until done to taste. Serve with the Chipotle Honey Sweet Potatoes and Brandied Grape Sauce.

Serves four

Wine Master's Suggestion: Biltmore Pinot Noir

Chipotle Honey Sweet Potatoes

1 chipotle chile in adobo sauce, puréed
1 cup (2 sticks) unsalted butter, softened
juice of 3 limes
1 tablespoon honey
1 tablespoon chopped cilantro
2 tablespoons salt
4 sweet potatoes

Combine the chipotle chile, butter, lime juice, honey, cilantro and salt in a bowl and mix well. Shape into logs and wrap in waxed paper. You can freeze this until needed and bring to room temperature before using.

Preheat the oven to 350 degrees. Place the sweet potatoes on a baking sheet and roast for 1 1/2 hours or until very tender and oozing natural sugar. Cool slightly and peel, discarding the skins. Mash the sweet potatoes with a fork in a large bowl. Add the butter mixture and mix well.

Serves four

Brandied Grape Sauce

1/2 cup coarsely chopped shallots
3 tablespoons chopped garlic
1/4 cup (1/2 stick) unsalted butter, melted
4 pounds seedless red grapes
1/2 cup cider vinegar
1 1/2 cups brandy
2 tablespoons all-purpose flour
1/2 gallon (8 cups) chicken stock
1/2 gallon (8 cups) veal stock
1 tablespoon chopped fresh rosemary
1/4 cup sugar
1/2 cup honey
1/2 cup heavy cream
salt and pepper to taste

Sauté the shallots and garlic in the butter in a saucepan. Add the grapes and cook until the grapes are lightly caramelized. Add the vinegar and brandy, stirring to deglaze the saucepan. Cook until reduced by 1/2. Add the flour and cook until bubbly, whisking constantly. Add the chicken stock and veal stock and cook until reduced by 1/2. Stir in the rosemary, sugar and honey.

Purée the mixture with an immersion blender. Add the cream and simmer for 15 minutes; season with salt and pepper. Strain the mixture into a bowl.

Serves six to eight

The Biltmore Kitchens

The preparation of elaborate meals for the Vanderbilts and their guests, as well as food for thirty to thirty-five servants, required three kitchens. Biltmore's Main Kitchen is a brightly lit room located in the Basement, just below the Breakfast Room. Its extra-large cook stove and steel storage cabinets were custom-made commercial-grade equipment designed to service a bustling work area.

In the Pastry Kitchen, the pastry chef baked breads and creates luncheon and dinner desserts and sweet treats for afternoon tea. It features a Bramhill, Deane & Co. oven as well as a Lorillard refrigerator to chill delicate pastry dough.

The Rotisserie Kitchen features a wood-fired oven with an electric spit; a rheostat mounted on the wall controlled its speed. Here poultry, hams, joints of beef, and wild game were roasted to perfection.

Chicken Potpie

A winter menu would not be complete without this traditional favorite. At the Stable Café, we serve our chicken potpie in individual soup bowls topped with a crisp crust.

3¹/2 pounds chicken legs, thighs and breasts
salt and pepper to taste
1 cup Biltmore Chardonnay Sur Lies
1 large onion, finely chopped
3 ribs celery, finely chopped
4 garlic cloves, minced
¹/4 cup (¹/2 stick) butter, melted
1 tablespoon chopped fresh sage
1 teaspoon dried oregano
1 teaspoon dried thyme
1 teaspoon dried basil
¹/3 cup all-purpose flour
¹/3 cup olive oil
1 quart (4 cups) chicken stock
1 cup heavy cream
1 (16-ounce) package frozen peas
2 sheets frozen pie or tart pastry, thawed

Preheat the oven to 275 degrees. Season the chicken with salt and pepper and place in an oiled roasting pan. Roast for 1 hour or until cooked through. Cool to room temperature and cut into bite-size pieces, discarding the skin and bones. Increase the oven temperature to 350 degrees.

Simmer the wine in a small saucepan until reduced by ¹/2. Sauté the onion, celery and garlic in the butter in a heavy saucepan over medium heat until the onion is translucent. Add the sage, oregano, thyme and basil and sauté for 1 minute. Add the flour and olive oil and stir to mix well. Cook for 1 minute.

Add the reduced wine, chicken stock and cream and bring to a simmer, stirring constantly. Stir in the chicken and peas and cook for 15 minutes or until thickened. Season with salt and pepper and cool. Spoon into 6 ovenproof bowls.

Cut the pie pastry into circles the diameter of the bowls. Place loosely over the chicken mixture in the bowls. Place on a baking sheet and bake for 25 minutes or until the crust is golden brown.

Serves six

Wine Master's Suggestion: Biltmore Chardonnay Sur Lies

Roasted Carolina Striped Bass with Crawfish Bread Pudding and Orange Butter

Crawfish Bread Pudding
1/2 cup chopped crawfish tail meat
1/4 cup finely chopped onion
1 tablespoon chopped garlic
1/4 cup finely chopped leek greens
1/4 cup finely chopped yellow bell pepper
1/4 cup finely chopped red bell pepper
1 tablespoon finely chopped shallot
2 croissants, cut into cubes
1 tablespoon chopped fresh thyme
1 tablespoon chopped fresh tarragon

2 tablespoons Cognac
2 eggs
1 cup heavy cream

Roasted Carolina Striped Bass
olive oil for searing
4 (6-ounce) striped bass fillets
salt and freshly ground white pepper
   to taste
Orange Butter (below)

For the bread pudding, preheat the oven to 325 degrees. Combine the crawfish meat with the onion, garlic, leek greens, yellow bell pepper, red bell pepper, shallot, croissants, thyme and tarragon in a large bowl. Add the brandy, eggs and cream and mix well. Let stand for 20 minutes to absorb the liquid.

Butter a baking dish or individual ramekins or spray with nonstick cooking spray. Spoon the pudding mixture into the prepared dish and place in a deeper pan. Add enough hot water to reach 3/4 of the way up the sides of the dish. Bake for 45 to 60 minutes or until set, depending on the size of the dish.

For the fish, heat a skillet over high heat and add a small amount of olive oil. Season the fish with salt and white pepper and place skin side up in the heated skillet. Sear until the fish releases from the pan, shaking slightly to test. Turn the fish over with a fish spatula and sear for 1 minute longer. Place the fish in a baking parchment-lined roasting pan and roast for 10 to 15 minutes or until cooked through.

To serve, cut the bread pudding into squares and place on serving plates or invert the individual puddings onto serving plates. Add the fish to the plates and spoon the Orange Butter over the top.

Serves four   *Wine Master's Suggestion*: Biltmore Signature Napa Valley Chardonnay

Orange Butter

2 shallots, minced
1 bay leaf
1/2 cup Biltmore Signature Napa Valley
   Chardonnay

1 cup freshly squeezed orange juice
31/2 cups (7 sticks) butter, chopped
1 tablespoon chopped chives

Combine the shallots and bay leaf with the wine in a saucepan and cook over medium-high heat until reduced by 1/4. Add the orange juice and cook until reduced by 1/4. Strain through a fine sieve into a clean saucepan and bring to a simmer. Reduce the heat and gradually whisk in the butter until incorporated. Stir in the chives and remove from the heat.

Makes three and one-half cups

Twenty-six guests celebrated the opening of Biltmore House on December 24, 1895. With so many people to see to, Biltmore's thirty to thirty-five domestic servants were kept very busy. The kitchens would have been especially hectic on Christmas Eve and Christmas Day, with the preparation of breakfasts served to guests in their rooms, luncheons, and two formal dinners. The aroma of roasting turkeys wafting through the first floor from the rotisserie in the basement ensured a table full of hungry guests.

Maine Lobster Frittata with Trout Caviar

1 (4- to 6-ounce) Maine lobster tail
2 tablespoons butter
1 cup finely chopped peeled Yukon Gold potato
1/4 cup chopped red bell pepper
salt and pepper to taste
1 tablespoon chopped fresh basil
4 eggs, beaten
trout caviar

Preheat the oven to 350 degrees. Boil the lobster tail in enough water to cover in a saucepan for 5 minutes. Drain and place in an ice bath immediately to cool. Hold the tail with the shell side down and cut through the shell with kitchen shears. Pull the meat from the shell and cut into small pieces, discarding the shell.

Melt the butter in a small nonstick ovenproof skillet. Add the potato and sauté until tender. Add the bell pepper and lobster meat and sauté for several minutes; season with salt and pepper. Add the basil and pour in the eggs. Cook over medium heat until halfway cooked; do not stir. Place in the oven and bake until the eggs are set. Cut into quarters and serve with trout caviar.

Serves two

Wine Master's Suggestion:
Biltmore Château Reserve Chardonnay

Warm Potato Salad

Savory, tart, and a little sweet, this potato salad is a perennial favorite at the Stable Café. It's especially good with a hearty sandwich such as a reuben.

    2 cups cider vinegar
    2 cups packed brown sugar
    8 cups water
    1/3 cup salt
    2 1/2 pounds unpeeled red potatoes,
        cut into 1-inch cubes
    8 ounces bacon, finely chopped
    1 1/2 cups sliced celery
    1 cup thinly sliced red onion
    2 tablespoons olive oil

Combine the vinegar, brown sugar, water and salt in a 2-qallon saucepan and bring to a boil. Add the potatoes and cook for 25 minutes or just until tender. Brown the bacon in a skillet. Combine the bacon, bacon drippings, celery, onion and olive oil in a bowl. Drain the potatoes and add to the bacon mixture. Mix gently and serve immediately.

Serves ten

The Butler's Staff

The head butler and under butlers served all meals, whether taken in the dining rooms or by tray in living rooms and bedrooms. They maintained china, crystal, and silver; set the tables; and plated food. The head butler oversaw the storage, decanting, and serving of wines. He used a grease pencil to write the evening's menu on porcelain tablets that were placed on the table to allow guests to see in advance what courses would be presented. Having the menu before them enabled guests to pace themselves during multicourse meals.

Christmas at Biltmore House

Biltmore House opened on Christmas Eve in 1895 to twenty-six members of Mr. Vanderbilt's family. A forty-foot evergreen in the Banquet Hall towered over a table piled with gifts. Stockings hung on mantles, plum pudding and minced pies were served, and 'Twas the Night Before Christmas was read to the children. The Asheville News and Hotel Reporter *noted:*

"The Imperial Trio furnished the music . . . and the rich costumes of the ladies, the soft lights, and the tastefully draped garlands of evergreen and mistletoe, interspersed with the shining leaves and red berries of the holly, created a scene beautiful to look upon."

Each year on Christmas morning, Mr. Vanderbilt invited estate workers and their families to a festive party in the Banquet Hall. Prestidigitators and Punch and Judy puppeteers provided entertainment. Refreshments included candy, cake, and ice cream, as well as oranges and bananas, which were rare winter treats. Everyone received a specially chosen gift. A receipt, dated December of 1898, from F.A.O. Schwartz department store in New York City and signed by Mrs. Vanderbilt, lists toy soldiers, jumping jacks, lanterns, tinsel stars, balloons, and jackstraws, as well as doctor, Indian, and baby dolls, all for the children. Adults received dress goods, gloves, and other useful items.

Creamy Horseradish Potatoes

2 tablespoons chopped shallots
2 tablespoons chopped garlic
1/4 cup prepared horseradish
2 tablespoons chopped fresh thyme
2 tablespoons chopped fresh rosemary
salt and freshly ground pepper to taste

3 cups heavy cream
6 baking potatoes, peeled and sliced
   1/8 inch thick
1/2 cup (2 ounces) finely grated
   Parmesan cheese

Preheat the oven to 350 degrees. Combine the shallots, garlic, horseradish, thyme, rosemary, salt and pepper in a bowl. Add the cream and mix well. Alternate layers of the potatoes and horseradish mixture in a baking dish with sides at least 2 inches deep until all the ingredients are used; press down to eliminate air pockets.

Cover with plastic wrap and foil and bake for 45 to 60 minutes or until the potatoes are tender. Remove the foil and plastic wrap and sprinkle with the Parmesan cheese. Bake just until the top is brown. Serve immediately.

Serves four or five

Parmesan Risotto

12 cups chicken stock
2 yellow onions, chopped
1/4 cup (1/2 stick) unsalted butter,
   melted
1 1/4 pounds uncooked arborio rice

1 cup Biltmore Château Reserve
   Chardonnay
salt and pepper to taste
1 cup (4 ounces) grated Parmesan cheese
1/4 cup (1/2 stick) unsalted butter

Heat the chicken stock in a saucepan and maintain at a low simmer. Sauté the onions in 1/4 cup butter in a saucepan over medium heat; do not brown. Add the rice and sauté for 8 to 12 minutes or until light golden brown. Add the wine, stirring to deglaze the saucepan. Cook until the liquid is reduced by 1/2.

Add the chicken stock 1/3 at a time, cooking until the liquid is nearly absorbed after each addition; the rice will be al dente. Season with salt and pepper and stir in the Parmesan cheese. Finish with 1/4 cup butter.

Serves six to eight

Homemade Cinnamon Rolls

1 1/2 cups warm water
1/4 cup sugar
1 envelope (2 1/4 teaspoons) quick-rising dry yeast
1 tablespoon vegetable oil
1 teaspoon salt
3 1/2 cups (or more) all-purpose flour
1 cup (2 sticks) unsalted butter, softened
2 tablespoons cinnamon
1 1/2 cups sugar

Mix the warm water and 1/4 cup sugar in a large mixing bowl. Sprinkle the yeast over the mixture and let stand until foamy. Stir in the oil and salt. Add the flour 1 cup at a time, mixing constantly with a dough hook to form a soft dough. Add additional flour if the dough is sticky.

Knead the dough for 10 minutes or until smooth and elastic. Place in a lightly oiled large bowl, turning to coat the surface. Let stand, covered with plastic wrap and a towel, in a warm place for 1 hour or until doubled in bulk.

Roll the dough gently to a 10×16-inch rectangle on a floured surface. Mix the butter, cinnamon and 1 1/2 cups sugar in a bowl and beat until smooth. Spread 1 cup of the butter mixture over the dough with a spatula. Roll the dough to form a log, enclosing the butter mixture; pinch the ends and seam to seal. Spread the remaining butter mixture in a 10×15-inch baking pan. Cut the log crosswise into 12 portions. Arrange evenly with the cut sides down in the prepared pan. Cover with plastic wrap and let rise for 30 minutes or until puffed.

Preheat the oven to 325 degrees. Bake the rolls for 35 minutes or until golden brown. Loosen the rolls from the edges of the pan with a sharp knife and place a large baking sheet over the pan. Invert the rolls onto the baking sheet. Serve warm.

Makes twelve

Pumpkin Pancakes with Toasted Pecan Butter

2 cups all-purpose flour
2 tablespoons baking powder
1 tablespoon baking soda
1/4 cup confectioners' sugar
1/4 teaspoon cinnamon
1/8 teaspoon nutmeg
1/2 teaspoon salt
3 eggs, beaten

1 cup buttermilk
1/2 cup milk
1/2 teaspoon vanilla extract
1/4 cup canned pumpkin
1 tablespoon butter, melted
1 tablespoon vegetable oil, or more
   as needed
Toasted Pecan Butter (below)

Whisk the flour, baking powder, baking soda, confectioners' sugar, cinnamon, nutmeg and salt together in a large mixing bowl. Combine the eggs, buttermilk, milk and vanilla in a medium bowl and mix until smooth. Add to the dry ingredients and whisk gently just until moistened. Whisk in the pumpkin and butter gently; do not overmix.

Heat a medium skillet over medium heat. Add 1 tablespoon vegetable oil and swirl the pan to coat evenly. Add 1/4 cup of the batter and cook until bubbles appear and the surface begins to look dry. Turn the pancake over and cook until golden brown. Adjust the heat if necessary for even browning and repeat with the remaining batter; add additional vegetable oil as needed. Serve with Toasted Pecan Butter, maple syrup and whipped cream.

Serves eight

Toasted Pecan Butter

3/4 cup (1 1/2 sticks) unsalted butter, softened
1/2 cup toasted pecan pieces
3 tablespoons maple syrup
1 teaspoon vanilla extract
1/2 teaspoon salt

Combine the butter, pecans, maple syrup, vanilla and salt in a mixing bowl and beat at medium speed until smooth. Remove to a sheet of plastic wrap with a rubber spatula and use the plastic wrap to shape the mixture into a log 1 inch in diameter. Chill until firm. Cut into medallions to serve.

Makes one cup

Choice Receipts

The left photograph is the cover of Choice Receipts, *which Biltmore's pastry chef used to prepare desserts for Biltmore House. It focused on chocolate desserts, "Specially Prepared for Walter Baker & Co.s. Exhibit at the World's Columbian Exposition 1893." Maria Parloa, columnist for* Ladies Home Journal *and founder of the Boston Cooking School, authored the pamphlet. Miss Parloa called chocolate a "perfect food . . . [for] those whose occupations oblige them to undergo severe mental strains." George Vanderbilt probably acquired the pamphlet at the exposition, which he attended.*

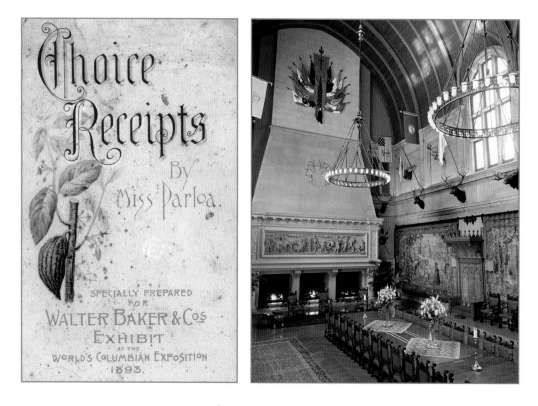

Banquet Hall

The Banquet Hall, reminiscent of a great medieval hall with its soaring seventy-foot ceiling, is the largest room in Biltmore House. Family and guests dined at a forty-foot oak table designed especially for the room. A door led to the hallway outside the Butler's Pantry, where food was plated and garnished before being served by liveried butlers.

In 1995, the room was the scene of a grand dinner celebrating Biltmore's first hundred years, given by the present owner, W.A.V. Cecil. On that occasion, the table was set with Printemps china by Herend, and Baccarat crystal chosen for the occasion.

Bread Pudding

Any bread, or even leftover cake, can be used for bread pudding.

3/4 cup (1 1/2 sticks) butter
1 3/4 cups heavy cream
2 1/4 cups milk
9 eggs
1 cup sugar
1/2 teaspoon cinnamon
1 tablespoon vanilla extract
3/4 loaf bread
Caramel Sauce (below)

Preheat the oven to 350 degrees. Combine the butter, cream and milk in a saucepan and heat almost to the boiling point, stirring to blend well. Beat the eggs with the sugar, cinnamon and vanilla in a bowl. Stir a small amount of the heated milk into the egg mixture, then stir the egg mixture into the heated milk.

Cut the bread into 1 1/2-inch cubes and sprinkle in a lightly greased 9×13-inch baking pan. Pour the milk mixture over the bread, coating evenly. Bake for 40 minutes or until set. Serve Caramel Sauce over the pudding.

Serves eight to twelve

Caramel Sauce

1 cup sugar
1 tablespoon lemon juice
1/4 cup water
2 tablespoons butter
1 cup heavy cream

Combine the sugar, lemon juice and water in a saucepan and mix well. Cook without stirring over medium-high heat until amber in color, using a wet pastry brush to wash the sugar crystals from the side of the pan. Remove from the heat and stir in the butter carefully until melted. Stir in the cream. Cool to room temperature.

Serves eight to twelve

The Breakfast Room

Although this room was called the Breakfast Room, breakfast was usually taken on trays in bedrooms. Family and guests gathered here at 1:30 for luncheons, seated around a large oval dining table in chairs upholstered in French silk velvet. Luncheons were less formal than dinners, but usually included five courses, beginning with fish, seafood, or a simple soup, and ending with puddings and custards, often featuring fruit. They provided an opportunity for everyone to gather and discuss their morning's activities and plan their afternoon adventures.

Old-Fashioned Molasses Cookies

2$^1/3$ cups all-purpose flour
1$^1/2$ teaspoons baking soda
1 teaspoon ground ginger
1 teaspoon ground cloves
1$^1/2$ teaspoons cinnamon
1 teaspoon salt
1 cup vegetable oil
$^1/3$ cup molasses
1$^1/3$ cups sugar
1 egg
sugar for coating

Preheat the oven to 350 degrees. Sift the flour, baking soda, ginger, cloves, cinnamon and salt together. Combine the oil, molasses, 1$^1/3$ cups sugar and the egg in a mixing bowl and beat at medium speed until smooth. Add the dry ingredients and mix well. Spoon into a covered container and chill in the refrigerator.

Scoop the mixture into balls the desired size and roll in sugar. Place on a cookie sheet sprayed with nonstick cooking spray. Bake for 10 minutes; do not overbake. Cool on the cookie sheet for several minutes and remove to a wire rack to cool completely. Serve immediately or freeze until ready to serve.

Makes twelve

Apple Gingerbread Cake

At the Bistro, we serve this with cinnamon ice cream and fresh cranberry sauce.

Apple Topping
3 or 4 apples, peeled, cored and
    thickly sliced
1/4 cup Apple Jack brandy
1 tablespoon lemon juice
1 cup sugar
1 tablespoon lemon juice
1/2 cup water
1 cup (2 sticks) butter, sliced

Cake
21/4 cups all-purpose flour
2 teaspoons baking cocoa
1/2 teaspoon baking soda

2 teaspoons ground ginger
11/2 teaspoons cinnamon
1/2 teaspoon ground cloves
1/2 teaspoon ground nutmeg
1/2 teaspoon ground allspice
1/2 teaspoon salt
1/2 cup (1 stick) butter, melted and cooled
3/4 cup molasses
3/4 cup sugar
1 tablespoon grated fresh ginger
1 egg, at room temperature
1/2 cup buttermilk, at room temperature
1/2 cup milk, at room temperature

For the topping, toss the apples with the brandy and 1 tablespoon lemon juice in a bowl. Combine the sugar, 1 tablespoon lemon juice and the water in a saucepan and cook until the mixture is a light caramel color. Add the butter and stir until the butter melts. Add the apples and cook until slightly tender. Cool to room temperature.

Line the bottom of a 8- or 9-inch round cake pan with baking parchment and grease the bottom and side of the pan. Arrange the apples in a fan pattern in the pan and pour the cooking syrup over the apples.

For the cake, preheat the oven to 350 degrees. Sift the flour, baking cocoa, baking soda, ground ginger, cinnamon, cloves, nutmeg, allspice and salt into a large bowl; make a well in the center.

Combine the butter, molasses, sugar and grated fresh ginger in a mixing bowl and mix with a paddle attachment. Whisk the egg, buttermilk and milk in a medium bowl. Add to the butter mixture, beating until smooth. Pour into the well in the dry ingredients and fold in gently.

Pour the batter over the apples in the prepared cake pan. Bake for 30 to 40 minutes or until a wooden pick inserted into the center comes out clean. Cool partially on a wire rack and loosen the edge with a spatula or small knife. Invert onto a serving plate.

Serves eight

Wine Master's Suggestion: Biltmore Century

Chocolate Truffle Financiers with Frangelico Sabayon

12 ounces semisweet chocolate
14 tablespoons butter
4 eggs
4 egg yolks
7 tablespoons sugar
3 tablespoons flour, sifted
Frangelico Sabayon (below)

Preheat the oven to 325 degrees. Spray muffin cups with nonstick cooking spray and coat with a mixture of equal parts flour and baking cocoa.

Melt the chocolate in a double boiler, whisking in the butter as the chocolate melts. Keep warm over hot water.

Combine the eggs, egg yolks and sugar in a mixing bowl and beat just until ribbons form; do not overmix. Add the flour and whisk until smooth. Fold the chocolate mixture gently into the egg mixture with a spatula. Spoon into the prepared muffin cups, filling to the bottom of the lip.

Bake for 10 to 15 minutes or until the cakes test done. Cool to room temperature in the muffin cups. Remove to serving plates and serve with Frangelico Sabayon.

Serves ten

Frangelico Sabayon

4 ounces white chocolate
1/2 cup egg yolks
1/3 cup sugar
2 tablespoons Frangelico
1/2 cup heavy whipping cream

Melt the white chocolate in a double boiler; keep warm over hot water. Combine the egg yolks, sugar and liqueur in a double boiler. Cook over medium-high heat for 8 to 10 minutes or until thickened and pale yellow, whisking constantly. Fold in the white chocolate; return the mixture to the heat if lumps form.

Whip the cream in a bowl until soft peaks form. Fold gently into the cooked mixture. Store in the refrigerator.

Serves ten

The Dairy

George Vanderbilt established a purebred Jersey herd to supply Biltmore House
with milk. The cows were so productive that Mr. Vanderbilt was urged to
sell his dairy products to the community. Early Biltmore Dairy products included
full-fat unpasteurized milk, butter, and vanilla and chocolate ice cream.
An early advertisement offered gallons of "pure" milk at 25 cents, sealed quart
bottles at 8 cents, sealed pints at 5 cents, and a pound of "gilt edge" butter
at 35 cents. Later items included fruit-flavored ice cream, popsicles, and seasonal
treats, such as molded Yule logs, Santa Clauses, and Thanksgiving motifs.

The above photograph is of Biltmore deliveryman Nathaniel Howard, c. 1906.
The Clydesdale horses that pulled the wagons wore rubber shoes
to keep the horses' hooves from waking sleeping customers in the wee hours
before dawn. The photo is donated by Mildred Dickerson Buchanan.

The families of people that worked at Biltmore Estate also enjoyed the
products from the purebred Jersey herd. Gladys Corn, daughter of blacksmith James
Fanning Corn, watched the cows being milked, milk cans being delivered, and
calves being fed. She recalled, "My sister Eva and I got to go to the Creamery every
day where we picked up our gallon of 'good ole Jersey milk.'" Milker Marion
McCarson's daughters Kathryn and Constance recalled that their father brought the
milk home in a galvanized pail. They drank the milk throughout much of
their childhood and assert, decades later, that they still have good teeth and bones.

Orange-Infused Vanilla Ice Cream

You will need an ice cream spinner for this recipe.

2¹/₂ cups heavy cream
1 cup half-and-half
¹/₂ cup sugar
1 vanilla bean, split
6 egg yolks, beaten
grated zest of 1 orange

Combine the cream, half-and-half, sugar and vanilla bean in a saucepan. Bring just to a simmer. Whisk a small amount of the heated mixture into the egg yolks, then whisk the egg yolks into the heated mixture. Cook until the mixture begins to thicken, stirring constantly. Whisk in the orange zest and remove the vanilla bean. Spoon into an ice cream spinner and freeze using the manufacturer's instructions.

Makes one and one-half to two quarts

Vanilla Pear Mimosa

1¹/₂ tablespoons (³/4 ounce) vanilla vodka
3 tablespoons (1¹/₂ ounces) pear nectar or pear juice
¹/₂ cup (4 ounces) Biltmore Methode Champenoise Sparkling Sec

Pour the vodka into a chilled Champagne flute. Top with the pear nectar and then the Champagne.

Serves one

Wine Appreciation

*W*hen the Vanderbilts and their friends dined at the Biltmore House, the standard was haute cuisine and bottles of fine wine. Today, Biltmore Estate wines are created in the same spirit, only gourmet fare isn't a necessity. Our wines complement tables ranging from simple to ambitious. No matter the varietal you choose, our wines pair particularly well with good conversation.

And while there are acknowledged customs regarding the pairing of food and wine, there are no hard-and-fast rules. There are, however, several things to consider when pairing wines with food.

Food and Wine Pairing

*W*ines get their names either from the grape that was used to make them (Chardonnay, Merlot, Cabernet Sauvignon) or the region in which they were made (Burgundy, Chianti, Sauternes). Generally, wine and food from

the same region can be a good pairing, like sausage with Riesling from Germany or pasta with Chianti from Italy. As wines become increasingly known by their grape variety rather than their region, you may want to experience a wine tasting or two to develop your own personal preferences.

The way a food is prepared is more important in determining the wine to be served than the food itself. For instance, try a light white wine such as Sauvignon Blanc with grilled chicken, but enjoy a full-bodied Chardonnay with chicken in cream sauce—and consider a rosé or red wine for chicken cooked with heavier Italian or Chinese flavors.

The simplest approach to food and wine pairing: When food and wines have similar flavors and characteristics, they won't overpower each other. This is why you might serve a sweet Sauternes with dessert. To match the tart flavors of feta cheese and garlic in popular Mediterranean dishes, an acidic wine such as Chardonnay is a good choice.

You may prefer to choose a wine that contrasts with your food. Salty dishes like smoked salmon are enhanced when served with a slightly sweet wine like a Riesling. Serve a light, acidic wine such as Sauvignon Blanc with a rich food like beef tenderloin with a cream sauce. Because alcohol accentuates heat, spicy foods also work well with slightly sweet wines because of their lower alcohol content.

Wine Tasting

Your sense of smell plays a major role in sampling and selecting wines. A wine's fragrance is called its nose, or bouquet. The scents you detect depend on the type of grape used, where it was grown, if the wine was aged in oak barrels, and how long it has been in the bottle.

Wines reveal their best qualities when served correctly. For example, wine must be served at optimum temperature, the cork extracted neatly, and the wine served in an appropriately shaped glass.

Some pointers:

TEMPERATURE CHECK: *Serve white wines just out of the refrigerator or slightly warmer; the sweeter the wine, the cooler the recommended serving temperature. Light, young red wines taste best between 55 and 60 degrees; full-bodied reds are typically enjoyed at 60 to 65 degrees. You can always start with wine a little too cold; it warms up quickly as a meal gets under way.*

SERVING SAVVY: *Wine should be opened gently, using an opener that enables you to extract the cork cleanly. Be sure to wipe off the rim of the bottle before serving the wine. If serving from the bottle, twist the bottle as you pour to prevent dripping. Fill a wine glass only one-half to two-thirds full (one-third for a wine tasting). Fine table wines come in a*

750-milliliter bottle, which is a little less than a quart and contains five to six glasses of wine. A split is a 375-milliliter half-bottle, perfect for an intimate occasion.

ORDER, ORDER: *If you're serving more than one wine with a meal, serve dry before sweet, white before red, light before full-bodied, and young before aged.*

THE TASTING: *To swirl and taste wine, grasp the stem of the glass rather than the bowl to avoid raising the wine's temperature. Set the glass on the table and swirl it cautiously. Then bring the glass quickly to your nose, breathe deeply, and savor a sip. Sample a variety of wines to familiarize yourself with all types.*

WINE GLASS CLASS: *Red wine glasses have larger bowls than white wine glasses. This allows more room for swirling so that you can enjoy the big bouquet that is the trademark of fine red wine. Ideally, a wine glass should be thin, with the rim of the glass as thin as the glass itself.*

GOOD TO THE LAST DROP: *Recork leftover wine and refrigerate it up to two days.*

In a Restaurant

In many restaurants, the waitstaff is coached on recommended wine pairings for specific menu items. Let them know your price range and what you are having for dinner. If you and your guests are eating different food, you can either compromise on a bottle of "all-purpose wine," such as a light red (not too sweet or too acidic), or order by the glass. A bottle is usually cheaper than buying by the glass.

When your server brings the bottle to your table, examine the label to verify it's what you ordered. If you are given the cork, make sure it isn't dried out or crumbly—a sign of improper storage or previous opening. Next, the server will pour a sip of wine. Swirl it around in the glass, smell it, and taste it. If it smells "off" or tastes vinegary, send it back—but don't return it just because you don't like it as much as you had hoped. After your approval, the waiter serves others at your table.

Taste and Aroma

Match all three of these white wines with most poultry, fish, and shellfish recipes, particularly grilled.

Chardonnay *is perhaps the most popular of all white wine grapes. It's generally a deep golden color, which hints that it has been aged in oak barrels. Usually dry, Chardonnay has buttery, fruity, vanilla, and toasty flavors. It pairs well with a host of entrées.*

Sauvignon Blanc *is a dry white wine that is lighter in color and body and more citrusy and herbaceous than Chardonnay. It is a food-friendly wine with an acidic zing.*

Riesling *is a light, fruity wine with a floral fragrance.*

Red wines aren't served just with red meats anymore. Find your preference.

Cabernet Sauvignon *is a deep, rich, ruby-red wine with peppery, berry, and vanilla qualities from oak aging. "Cab" is a big, full-bodied, and intense wine. It pairs well with beef, poultry, pasta, and game meats.*

Merlot *also has a deep ruby color and is a softer, more supple red wine than Cab. Its flavor can hint of berry, black cherry, plum, spice, and tobacco. It pairs well with poultry and lamb.*

Pinot Noir *is more delicate than the two reds listed above. Hints of spicy cherries with earthy nuances create a complex flavor. It pairs well with beef and ham.*

Biltmore Wines

Château Reserve Collection

CHÂTEAU RESERVE CHARDONNAY
Fermented and aged in small, medium-toasted oak barrels, this white wine presents a complex aroma. Serve chilled with salads, chicken, and pasta. It goes well with cream sauces.

CHÂTEAU RESERVE CLARET
This unique blend of grapes, barrel aged in French Oak, makes for a wonderful red French-style wine. Paired with grilled beef and red sauces, it makes for a palate pleaser.

CHÂTEAU RESERVE CABERNET SAUVIGNON
This is a full-bodied, well-balanced red wine. This oak-aged wine is great now or will age gracefully. It will pair with venison, lamb, and red meat.

CHÂTEAU RESERVE CABERNET FRANC
A wonderful easy-sipping red wine! Aged in French Oak with a silky finish, it complements a variety of foods and stands well by itself.

Sparkling Wines

CHÂTEAU RESERVE METHODE CHAMPENOISE BLANC DE BLANC BRUT
Brilliant and luminous with tiny bubbles, this world-class wine offers autumnal aroma while honey, citrus, and mint flavors linger in a buttery finish. It is an outstanding dinner wine, bringing perfection to every meal.

CHÂTEAU METHODE CHAMPENOISE BRUT
This sparkling wine is our finest offering in the elegant French tradition. Brilliant and luminous with tiny bubbles, this is truly a world-class wine. The Château Methode Champenoise is an outstanding dinner wine that can be enjoyed with every meal.

METHODE CHAMPENOISE SPARKLING SEC
Slightly sweeter than brut sparkling wines. Perfect for occasions of every type, this Sec is also well suited for brunch or accompanying cold foods and desserts.

METHODE CHAMPENOISE BLANC DE BLANC BRUT
Delicate aromas and fruity taste. An award-winning classic with fine bubbles. The Blanc de Blanc Brut is a delicious wine with a good acidic background.

METHODE CHAMPENOISE BLANC DE NOIR BRUT
This light pink wine, made from Pinot Noir grapes, is well balanced with a lingering citrus taste. Great with turkey, tuna, or grilled meats.

METHODE CHAMPENOISE PAS DE DEUX SEC
This is our sweetest sparkling! A blend of nontraditional grapes makes this a fun, any-occasion sipping pleasure.

Red Wines

MERLOT
This balanced, medium-bodied red wine has soft tannins. Rich and elegant, it pairs well with a variety of red meats and cheeses.

CABERNET SAUVIGNON
Spicy fruit aromas and a long-lasting, mild oak finish mark this full-bodied red wine. This wine has a good aging potential or can be enjoyed now. It complements any type of red meat.

CARDINAL'S CREST (OUR UNIQUE BLEND)
This selection is named after ceremonial wall hangings of the seventeenth-century French statesman Cardinal Duc de Richelieu in Biltmore's collection. A blend of several grapes, it pairs with veal, casseroles, and Indian dishes.

PINOT NOIR
This soft, velvety wine is wonderful for sipping but pairs well with meats and hearty fish.

SANGIOVESE (MAIN GRAPE OF CHIANTI)
A well-structured wine with smoky tones. Serve with steaks, eggplant Parmesan, or spaghetti and meatballs.

RED CENTURY
A dry but fruity blend of Sangiovese and Merlot grapes. Nice, medium-bodied, and well balanced. Delicious wine with meats and Italian dishes.

SYRAH (ALSO KNOWN AS SHIRAZ)
This is a rich wine with silky textures and a long-lasting finish. Pair with beef, hearty foods, and spicy dishes.

LIMITED RELEASE MERLOT
(BARREL AGED IN FRENCH AND AMERICAN OAK)
Spicy fruit aromas and a long-lasting finish characterize this full-bodied, velvety wine. Enjoy with any meat dish.

RED ZINFANDEL
A nicely balanced wine ready to enjoy. The oak aging has softened the flavors, and it pairs well with red meats and game birds.

Signature Wines and Antler Hill

NORTH COAST CABERNET SAUVIGNON
This dark cherry-colored wine will fill your senses and entice your palate! Pairs well with red meats, lamb, and your favorite hearty meatloaf.

NORTH COAST SYRAH
Nice fruit! Wonderful with veal, your favorite pad-thai, or roast duck.

NAPA VALLEY CHARDONNAY
This balanced white wine is delicious with seafood, salads, salmon, and poultry.

ANTLER HILL CABERNET SAUVIGNON
Carefully chosen by our winemakers and from our best grower in California comes this wonderful wine. Ready to enjoy now or, with its good aging potential, for future enjoyment!

White Wines

SAUVIGNON BLANC
A classic dry, crisp white wine, full-bodied with a pleasant finish. It is particularly pleasing with fish, shrimp, and shellfish.

CHARDONNAY SUR LIES
This dry style of wine is aged on its sediment, or "lies," to create more complex flavors. The aging process lends freshness of fruit to this pleasantly light wine.

DRY RIESLING
A pleasant dry taste of fruit that pairs well with goat cheese, blue cheese, and Asian foods. Enjoy this nice surprise!

CHENIN BLANC
Delicate flavors make this a fresh and fruity wine. It is ideal by itself or as a companion to desserts.

CENTURY
A delightful blend of Riesling, Gewürztraminer, and Muscat Canelli. This semisweet wine can be served as an aperitif, with light desserts, or with fresh fruits.

PINOT GRIGIO
This dry white wine has a citrus and spicy finish. It is a refreshing companion to salmon and other seafood entrées.

VIOGNIER
An unusual medium-bodied wine with a delicate finish that boasts a floral bouquet. Enjoy its refined character with salmon, lobster, or crawfish.

WINEMAKER'S SELECTION CHENIN BLANC
Sweet spice and tropical flavors make this sweet wine vibrant and lively. Pair it with desserts or fruit to enjoy its lingering flavors.

LIMITED RELEASE SAUVIGNON BLANC
This Sauvignon Blanc receives its distinctive characteristics from a second fermentation that takes place in oak barrels, resulting in a soft and supple dinner wine. A wonderful accompaniment to seafood dishes.

Rosé Wines

ZINFANDEL BLANC DE NOIR ("WHITE ZINFANDEL")
This pleasant semisweet rosé wine has a lively flavor and is easy to enjoy with pizza and picnic foods.

CABERNET SAUVIGNON BLANC DE NOIR
The delicate floral aroma and refreshing fruity flavor of this semisweet rosé goes well with Asian cuisine. Serve well chilled.

Wine and Food Pairing Chart

FOOD	WINES
Hot, spicy foods *Ingredients like:* chiles, ginger, and pepper *Common cuisines:* Chinese, Indian, Mexican, and Thai	**Slightly sweet, fruity, light wines** such as *Burgundy*, Chenin Blanc, Gamay Beaujolais, Gewürztraminer, Pinot Noir, Riesling, *Rhone wines*, and light Zinfandels
Acidic, tart foods *Ingredients like:* feta cheese, garlic, lemon, tomatoes, vinegar, and citrus *Common cuisines:* Creole, Greek, Italian, and Japanese	**High-acid wines** such as Chardonnay, *Chianti*, Sauvignon Blanc, and sparkling whites
Rich foods *Ingredients like:* butter, cheese, lobster, red meats, and salmon *Common cuisines:* French, German, Italian, and Southern	**Acidic, citrus wine** such as Sauvignon Blanc **Oaky, toasty, buttery wine** such as Chardonnay **Tannic (tart), darker reds** like Cabernet Sauvignon, Merlot, and dark Zinfandel
Salty or smoked foods *Ingredients like:* olives, salt-cured or smoked meats, and soy sauce *Common cuisines:* Japanese, German, Greek, and Southern	**Slightly sweet, fruity light wines** such as Chenin Blanc, Gamay Beaujolais, Gewürztraminer, Pinot Noir, Riesling, sparkling wine, and light Zinfandels
Sweet foods *Ingredients like:* coconut, corn, fruits, mint, and thyme *Common cuisines:* Chinese, French, Indian, and Thai	**For foods other than desserts: slightly sweet wines** such as Chenin Blanc, Riesling, and Gewürztraminer **For desserts: sweet wines** such as Madeira, Ruby Port, *Sauternes*, sherry, and sparkling wines such as Asti Spumante

Note: Pair sweet foods with sweet wines, but the food should never be sweeter than the wine.

(Those wines listed by grape variety are in roman type; regional wines are in italic.)

Bibliography

Advertisement for Biltmore Apiary. *Asheville Daily Citizen.* August 24, 1896.

"A Pretty Romance." *New York World.* May 29, 1898.

Beeton, Isabella. *The Book of Household Management.* 1861. United States: Farrar, Straus and Giroux, 1969.

Biltmore Estate Oral History Project. Biltmore Estate Archives. Eugenia Halyburton Chandler, Sarah Drake Lanning, Mildred Vanderhoof Glenn, Ruby Redmon Faulkner/Redmon Brothers, Mildred Dickerson Buchanan, George Marsden Wallis, Houston Ray Henson, Belle Taylor Ballard, Annie Saulters, Essie Smith Kuykendal Copeland, Annie Matilda Scarbrough, William Cogburn, Agnes Duke Todd, Ellen Davis Johnson, Herman and Ruby Gaddy, Mary Ellen Faulkner and Cora Shillinglaw Kuykendall, James Charles Berry, James Fanning Corn, and Marion McCarson.

Biltmore Farms Letterhead. Biltmore Estate Archives.

"Biltmore House Formally Opened." *Asheville News and Hotel Reporter.* December 25, 1895.

Biltmore House Guest Book. Biltmore Estate Archives.

Bureau of the Census. 1900 *(Biltmore Precinct).* Washington, D.C.

Carter, Mary Elizabeth. *Millionaire Households and Their Domestic Economy with Hints Upon Fine Living.* New York: D. Appleton & Company, 1903.

Correspondence. Morten & Co., Wine Merchants and Importers, New York, New York. 1908 and 1913. Superintendents' Office Records. Biltmore Estate Archives.

Davidson, Alan. *The Oxford Companion to Food.* New York: Oxford University Pess, 1999.

"Employees Give Ice Cream Cake Dateline 1925." *Old Asheville Gazette.* August 1925.

Escoffier, Georges Auguste. *Le Guide Culinaire, The Complete Guide to the Art of Modern Cookery,* first published in 1907. Trans. H. L. Cracknell and R. F. Kaufmann. New York: Mayflower Books, 1921.

"Farewell to '95: Gay Scenes Usher in the New Year at Biltmore House." *Asheville Daily Citizen.* January 1, 1896.

"Farmer Vanderbilt." *Asheville News and Hotel Reporter,* Vol. 5, No. 4 (February 20, 1897).

"Festive Birthday Celebration for Mrs. John F. A. Cecil Dateline 1925." *The Old Asheville Gazette.* August 1925.

"From His Country Boys, Vanderbilt Got a Lot of Conservation Ideas." *Asheville Times.* December 1, 1958.

Garrett, Theodore Francis, ed. *Encyclopaedia of Practical Cookery.* London: L. Upcott Gill, 1898.

Herman, Eli, Kitchen Garden Manager, Biltmore Estate. "The Kitchen Garden." July 2003. Museum Services Reference Files.

History and Collections Reference Files. Museum Services. Biltmore Estate.

House, B. F. "Camping Outfit." May 22, 1894.

Kasson, John F. *Rudeness and Civility: Manners in 19th Century Urban America.* New York: The Noonday Press, 1990.

Katsigianis, Ted, Vice President of Agricultural Services, Biltmore Estate. "Contemporary Agriculture—Biltmore Estate." July 15, 2003. Museum Services Reference Files.

McNamee, Charles to Messrs. Phipps & Pinous. November 22, 1902. Biltmore Estate Archives.

McNamee, Charles to Thomas Morch. December 14, 1895. Biltmore Estate Archives.

McNamee, Theodore H., Esq. to Charles McNamee. November 7, 1902. Biltmore Estate Archives.

Memorandum. Charles McNamee to George Vanderbilt. June 8, 1894. Biltmore Estate Archives.

Memorandum. J. Lenton to Charles McNamee. June 8, 1896. Biltmore Estate Archives.

"Menu Book, Biltmore House, 1904." Biltmore Estate Archives. Donated by Mr. Mark Barabas, whose mother, Esther Anderson, was a cook in Biltmore House.

Merrill, Pauline to Mrs. T. S. Viele. Buffalo, New York. March 1905.

Note. B. L. House to Edward Harding. May 22, 1894. Biltmore Estate Archives.

Parloa, Maria. Choice Receipts. Dorchester, MA: Walter Baker & Co., 1892.

Paston-Williams, Sarah. *The Art of Dining: A History of Cooking and Eating.* London: The National Trust, 1993.

Receipt. Alfred Bartino & Son, Wholesale & Export Grocers, Wine and Spirit Merchants, Southampton, England. June 24, 1897. Biltmore Estate Archives.

Receipt. Christmas Tree Fund. F. A. O. Schwartz, New York, NY. December 19, 1895. Biltmore Estate Archives.

Receipt. Food. J. M. Heston & Son, Confectioners and Bakers, Asheville, NC. January 1, 1902 and May 4, 1905. W. M. Hill, Asheville Fish Company, French Bakery, G. A. Greer, Frank O'Donnell, Bonanza Wine & Liquor Company. Biltmore Estate Archives.

Receipt. J. W. Hampton, Jr. & Co., Customs Brokers and Forwarders, New York, May 24, 1895. Biltmore Estate Archives.

Receipts. Seed Purchases. Biltmore Estate Archives.

Receipts. Silver. Edward Tessier, Manufacturing Jeweller [sic] and Silversmith, 26 New Bond Street, London. Biltmore Estate Archives.

Receipts. Travel. George Vanderbilt. Hotel Bristol, Paris. June 22–17, 1891; and Princes Restaurant, Ltd. June 18, 1897. Biltmore Estate Archives.

"Report Comparing Harvests, 1892, 1893, 1894." Biltmore Estate Archives.

Sambrook, Pamela A. and Peter Brears. *The Country House Kitchen 1659–1900.* London: Sutton Publishing in Association with the National Trust, 1997.

Schenck, Dr. Carl to George Vanderbilt. October 11 [no year]. Biltmore Estate Archives.

Vanderbilt, Edith. Dinner Book. Biltmore Estate Archives.

Vanderbilt, Gertrude. Dinner Book. Archives of American Art. Smithsonian Institution. Washington, D.C.

"Vanderbilts Go Fishing." *New York Times.* July 5, 1908.

Weston, George to Charles McNamee. August 10, 1896. Biltmore Estate Archives.

Weston, George to Charles McNamee. January 16, 1896. Biltmore Estate Archives.

Weston, George to Charles McNamee. October 6, 1896. Biltmore Estate Archives.

Wheeler, Anna [Mrs. Arthur]. "Mrs [sic] George W. Vanderbilt." [no date].

Willey, Day Allen. "Vanderbilt of the Mountain." *New York Ladies World.* September 1909.

Williams, Susan. *Savory Suppers and Fashionable Feasts.* New York: Pantheon Books, in association with the Strong Museum, 1985.

Zieman, Hugo and Mrs. F. L. Gillette. *The White House Cookbook.* New York: The Saalfield Publishing Company, 1901.

Index

181